PRIDE OF THE SOUTH

A SOCIAL HISTORY OF SOUTHERN ARCHITECTURE

BY WAYNE ANDREWS

NEW YORK ATHENEUM *1979*

FOR VIRGINIA CHILDS HODGES

"*A man will talk about how he'd like to escape from living folks. But it's the dead folks that do him the damage. It's the dead ones that lay quiet in one place and don't try to hold him, that he can't escape from.*"

LIGHT IN AUGUST, *William Faulkner*

Library of Congress Cataloging in Publication Data

Andrews, Wayne.
    Pride of the South.

    Bibliography: p.
    Includes index.
    1. Architecture—Southern States.   2. Architecture
and society—Southern States.   I. Title.
NA720.A5   1979   720'.975   78-3214
ISBN 0-689-10931-8 (clothbound)
ISBN 0-689-70579-4 (paperback)

Published simultaneously in Canada by McClelland and Stewart Ltd.
Composed by American-Stratford Graphic Services, Inc.,
Brattleboro, Vermont
Printed and bound by Halliday Lithograph Corporation, West Hanover and
Plimpton, Massachusetts
Designed by Harry Ford
First Edition

PROLOGUE

The South is a place, but a place whose address seems to have been recently mislaid. This is another way of saying that the tried and true clichés about the South with which we grew up are no longer valid, and that we are not too sure as yet about the clichés that are coming into favor. This might suggest that there is a need at the moment for an encyclopedic account of Southern architecture. This is a need that I have no intention of of fulfilling. To begin with, I have virtually eliminated the seventeenth century for the to me quite adequate reason that there was not enough prosperity in those years to allow for more than mere building. I have also chosen to emphasize the extraordinary at the expense of the ordinary.

All architecture is a stage set, and most architectural historians spend most of their time on the set itself, on the problem of design and on the history of architectural ideas. This has not been my aim in *Pride of the South*. My ambition has been to sketch the scene in which the stage was set: where the money came from is important, and so are the clients who gave the architects their chance. You may be disappointed to find that not every client stands completely revealed. So am I. I should like to place the blame for this failing on the Civil War, or, rather, on the overemphasis on the War. The War has attracted and continues to attract the attention of historians who might better have spent their time writing biographies of planters or businessmen.

The South is a vast area, but not so vast as to be devoid of characteristics. First of all, it was and remains mostly a rural civilization, in spite of the growth of cities like Atlanta. Ideas are not likely to travel as fast in a rural as in an industrial world, and it is true that Southern architecture, aside from the innovations of Thomas Jefferson, tends to be more conservative than that of the North. There is nothing reprehensible about this. Nor is there anything reprehensible about the Southern love of luxury. When the South had money to spend, it spent it, often in a manner that alarmed visitors from New England.

And now I must mention one complication: the New South proclaimed by Henry W. Grady in 1886. It was Grady's hope that the South would catch up with the economic development of the North. The South that he yearned for was that which Henry M. Flagler envisioned when he built the Ponce de León Hotel in Saint Augustine and extended his railway system to Key West. It was also the South that tempted John D. Rockefeller, Jr. to invest so many millions in the restoration of Colonial Williamsburg.

We are still living with the consequences of the work of Flagler and Rockefeller and we must face the fact that a certain confusion obtains in the South of 1979. A state of confusion may not be ideal, but confusion has always been the penalty paid for breathing. Please keep this in mind when I urge you, as I shall, to remember that John C. Portman's Hyatt Regency Hotel in Atlanta is as *southern* in its way as the Westover of William Byrd II.

ACKNOWLEDGMENTS

This book has been over thirty years in the making, and so many people have been helpful—so many have opened doors or given me a lift—that I may, inadvertently have forgotten some one who went out of his or her way. But I must remember to thank Captain and Mrs. R. K. Anderson of Stateburg, Stephan J. Blaut of Luray, the late Theodore Bolton of New York, the late Henry I. Brock of the *New York Times*, Alan Burnham of Greenwich, Mr. and Mrs. Richard Childress of Miami, Mr. and Mrs. St. Julien Ravenel Childs of Charleston, the late Gifford A. Cochran of New York, Mr. and Mrs. Walter Creese of Urbana, Mr. and Mrs. Larry Curry of Pacific Palisades, Mrs. Jane Davies of New York, W. M. Davis, Jr. of Savannah, Dr. and Mrs. Hilbert DeLawter of Charlottesville, Leonard K. Eaton of Ann Arbor, W. Hawkins Ferry of Grosse Pointe, Mr. and Mrs. Roy P. Frangiamore of Atlanta, the staff of the Galveston Historical Foundation, the Reverend and Mrs. Julien Gunn of Nashville, Mrs. Robert Hagerty of Charleston, the late Talbot F. Hamlin of New York, Mr. and Mrs. Harwell Hamilton Harris of Raleigh, Miss Emilie V. Haynsworth of Auburn, F. Burrall Hoffman of Hobe Sound, Mr. and Mrs. Graham Hood of Williamsburg, Mrs. Patricia LaLand of Williamsburg, Clay Lancaster of Nantucket, Grady McWhiney of the University of Alabama, Peter Manigault of Charleston, Chapman J. Milling of Sumter, Mr. and Mrs. Robert D. Orr, Jr., of Palm Beach, W. L. Pressly of the Atlanta Historical Society, Mr. and Mrs. Edward Rawson of Bethesda, Hugh Samper of Williamsburg, Mrs. Susan Schaal of Boca Raton, Miss Carolyn Schwager of Savannah, Albert Simons of Charleston, Goldwin Smith of Grosse Pointe, Mrs. Robert D. Stecker of Dallas, the late Samuel G. Stoney of Charleston, Charles C. Wall and his staff at Mount Vernon, Miss Martha White of Stateburg, Philip L. White of Austin, Samuel Wilson, Jr. of New Orleans, Mr. and Mrs. Thomas B. Winston of Washington, Mr. Willis F. Woods of Seattle, and Wayne Yenawine of Columbia. Plus a special salute to Miss Julia Reynolds of Sumter.

The Houdon bust of Jefferson is reproduced courtesy of Boston Museum of Fine Arts. The other negatives are my own. But I must express my gratitude to Dick Schuler who has developed and enlarged my negatives for so many years and given me priceless advice. Last of all, my thanks to Harry Ford of Atheneum, without whose pains this book would not look the way it should and does.

CONTENTS

THE LOWER SOUTH, 60

THE DEEP SOUTH, 105

x   *Contents*

PRIDE OF
THE SOUTH

Marble bust of Thomas Jefferson. 1789 (Jean-Antoine Houdon). Courtesy Museum of Fine Arts, Boston.

THE UPPER SOUTH

Nostalgia may be the most famous of all Southern crops, but it is not the only crop, as a glance at the career of Thomas Jefferson will prove. To him the past was not sacrosanct: he preferred to gamble on the future. "No society can make a perpetual constitution or even a perpetual law," he reminded Madison in the fall of 1789. "The earth belongs always to the living generation."

The Declaration of Independence that he drafted was a dangerous document, promising with its stress on natural rights a perpetual revolution. This could not have alarmed him. "There is," he one day told his daughter who was struggling with her studies, "something in the American character which regards nothing as desperate."

An architect in his own right, he saw no reason why America should not lead the world in architecture. "I am an enthusiast on the subject of the arts," he admitted. "But it is an enthusiasm of which I am not ashamed, as its object is to improve the taste of my countrymen, to increase their reputation, to reconcile to them the respect of the world, and to procure them its praise." There is a formality to Jefferson's prose which may put off Americans who fail to reckon with the world from which he came. He was a farmer—let us dismiss the romantic rhetoric which has turned the plantations of eighteenth-century Virginia into so many noble sites—and spoke with caution as he penetrated the great world of his era.

As any innovator should have been, he was ashamed of the standards of the Virginia of his childhood. "The genius of architecture seems to have shed its maledictions over this land," he commented in the *Notes on Virginia*. "Buildings are often erected by individuals, of considerable expense. To give them symmetry and taste would not increase their cost. It would only change the arrangement of the materials, the form and combination of the members. This would often cost less than the burthen of barbarous ornament with which these buildings are sometimes charged. But the first principles of the art are unknown, and there exists scarcely a model among us sufficiently chaste to give us an idea of them."

While Minister to France he found one chaste model in the Maison Carrée at Nîmes. "Here I am, Madam, gazing whole hours at the Maison Carrée like a lover at his mistress," he wrote his good friend the Comtesse de Tessé. "The stocking-weavers and silk-spinners around it consider me a hypochondriac Englishman, about to write with a pistol the last chapter of his history. This is the second time I have been in love since I left Paris. The first was with a Diana at the Château de Laye-Epinaye in Beaujolais, a delicious morsel of sculpture by M.-A. Slodtz. This, you will say, was in rule, to fall in love with a female beauty; but with a house! It is out of all precedent. No, Madam, it is not without a precedent in my own history. While in Paris, I was violently smitten with the Hôtel de Salm, and used to go to the Tuileries almost daily to look at it. The *loueuse de chaises*, inattentive to my passion, never had the complaisance to place a chair there, so that, sitting on a parapet, and twisting my neck around to see the object of my admiration, I generally left it with a *torti-colli*."

Jefferson may be accused of casting a backward glance at the Maison Carrée, but his purpose in studying this Roman monument of 16 B.C. was revolutionary. For three hundred years or more architects had assumed that the founders of the Renaissance had given the final interpretation of the legacy of the Ancient World. By examining so closely an actual Roman building Jefferson was undermining the authority of the Renaissance and so was leading us toward modern architecture.

This, he decided, must be the model for the new Capitol of Virginia that he was designing with the assistance of the French architect Charles-Louis Clérisseau. He was displeased to learn that the people of Richmond were about building the Capitol without listening to his advice. "Pray try if you can to effect the stopping of this work," he urged. "How is a taste for this beautiful art to be formed in our countrymen unless we avail ourselves of every occasion when public buildings are erected of presenting them models for their study and imitation?"

Although the façade was not stuccoed over until 1798, the cornerstone of the Capitol was laid in 1785. Here was the first public building in the temple style in the modern world, begun twenty-three years before Vignon went to work on the next example, the Church of the Madeleine in Paris.

As a tourist in France Jefferson was as curious as he was diligent. When not assembling his collection of Houdon busts and urging on the sculptor's commission to portray Washington, he managed to make himself an expert on the last word in French architecture. Besides inspecting Pierre Rousseau's Hôtel de Salm (today the Palace of the Legion of Honor), he made his way with his charming friend Maria Cosway to Bagatelle, the splendid residence in the Bois that Bélanger had designed for Louis XVI's brother the Comte d'Artois. He also set off with Mrs. Cosway for Le Désert, the estate at Chambourcy of a commissioner of waterworks, where there was a house disguised as a ruined column. "How grand the idea excited by the remains of such a column!" he exclaimed. But he may have enjoyed most of all the pavilion at Louveciennes of Madame du Barry. This was the creation of Claude-Nicolas Ledoux, whose imperious tollhouses surrounding Paris were to be rediscovered and appreciated by the connoisseurs of the twentieth century.

In England Jefferson found less to admire. "I fancy," he concluded, "it must be the quantity of animal food eaten by the English, which renders their character unsusceptible of civilization." In any event their recent buildings were disappointing. "Their architecture," he reported in the spring of 1786, "is in the most wretched style I ever saw, not to except America, where it is bad, nor even Virginia, where it is worse than in any other part of America which I have seen."

Bored he may have been by the achievements of the Adam brothers and their contemporaries, but he was aware of one English contribution to civilization. "The gardening in that country is the article in which it surpasses all the earth," he admitted. "I mean their pleasure gardening. This, indeed, went far beyond my ideas." He stopped at Pain's Hill where Charles Hamilton's Gothic temple by Batty Langley may have reminded him of that "small Gothic temple of antique appearance" he had dreamed of erecting in a burying place near Monticello. He also visited Lord Cobham's grounds at Stowe where he suffered through John Adams's insufferable comments. "The temples to Bacchus and Venus are quite unnecessary," Adams maintained, "as mankind have no need of artificial incitement to such amusements. The temples of Ancient Virtue, of the British Worthies, of Friendship, of Concord are in a higher taste," he conceded, adding that "it will be long, I hope, before ridings,

parks, pleasure grounds and ornamented farms grow so much in fashion in America."

We do not know how long Jefferson paused at Chiswick, but since this was close as he ever came to a Palladian villa, and he adored Palladio, this must have been his most satisfying moment in Great Britain. Monticello, the mansion he had begun building in 1770, was to be transformed into a Palladian temple on his return to America. While he took pains with such details as miniature dumb-waiters, and was careful to tuck all stairways out of sight, the grand design that finally emerged owed much to what William Kent and his patron the Earl of Burlington had wrought at Chiswick in the 1720s.

Palladio! Palladio! The sixteenth-century Italian architect had reproduced the Maison Carrée in Book IV of his publications. And Palladio was very much in Jefferson's mind when he laid out Poplar Forest in 1806, his retreat near Lynchburg. In 1817, eight years after Monticello was completed, he was still a Palladian when he began planning the campus of the University of Virginia.

"This letter is that of a friendly beggar," he wrote Benjamin Henry Latrobe, the chief architect of the Capitol in Washington, praying he would send on a few ideas for the pavilions and dormitories of the new University at Charlottesville. No ordinary pavilions would do: they "should be models of taste and correct architecture, and of a variety of appearance, no two alike, so as to serve as specimens of orders for the architectural lectures."

Latrobe took the liberty of suggesting a Palladian precedent for the Corinthian columns of Pavilion III, the most expensive of all ten, and may have indicated that the Pantheon in Rome would be a fine model for the Rotunda or Library.* But the scheme of the University was Jefferson's own. He could not fail to pay his respects to Ledoux. This he accomplished in the façade for Pavilion IX, tactfully echoing the rear elevation of Ledoux's hôtel in Paris for Mademoiselle Guimard the dancer. With the Capitol in Richmond, and Monticello, the University proves Jefferson's

---

* Jefferson might have been appalled by the reverence of certain members of the faculty in 1979. Deeply distressed by the liberties taken by Stanford White when he restored the Rotunda in 1895 following a fire, they insisted that there should be a remodeling eliminating every trace of White's work. As a matter of fact, White was guilty of nothing more reprehensible than improving on Jefferson: he dared to remove the second story floor, opening up the building to the splendid height of the dome. Jefferson might have been the first to salute this feat.

claim to be as commanding in architecture as in politics.

Not that Jefferson had everything his own way on the Board of Visitors. One of his colleagues was the choleric planter John Hartwell Cocke. Well aware that "slavery is the great cause of all the great evils in our land," Cocke was in favor of shipping all Negroes back to Africa. He had ideas on almost any subject. Virginia should stop raising tobacco, he insisted, and when he was not promoting Bible, Tract and Sunday School societies, stood firm for universal prohibition. Nor was he pleased for long with the administration of the University, which he likened to a "school of infidelity." The students alarmed him: he never knew what they were plotting behind Jefferson's serpentine walls. There was no doubt "the young men found ready at hand the most extraordinary facilities for giving annoyance and also for escaping after it." The faculty was partly to blame, he reasoned, and he fumed at the appointment of Thomas Cooper, suspected of being a Unitarian or worse, to be professor of chemistry. "Do save us from this inundation of foreigners," he grumbled, recalling that Cooper was a native of England. No wonder Cocke was dogmatic on the subject of architecture. No ornament should be tolerated on any university building, he argued, and he pronounced Jefferson's designs a "raree show."

Jefferson was so patient in his dealings with Cocke and Adams that you might suppose that he had the sophistication of an aristocrat. But he did not come from aristocratic stock, even if one of the Randolphs on his mother's side had been knighted for his legal services to the colony. The Jeffersons, like the founders of so many great American families, climbed in the New World above their humble origins in the Old. In fact, these founders were so eager to rise that they may be best understood as so many prisoners of the certainties of the eighteenth century anxious to escape into the uncertainties of the nineteenth. The legend of the cavaliers, of the highborn progenitors of the First Families of Virginia is no more than a legend.

Unremarkable indeed was the origin of the Carter dynasty. John, the first of the line, who showed up in Virginia toward 1649, came from no one knows where, but by 1657 was a member of the Governor's Council and by his death in 1669 was worth 2,250 pounds. His son Robert, nicknamed the "King," understood, as his father did not, how to make the most of his opportunities. When he died in 1732 he left 300,000 acres, 1,000 slaves and 10,000 pounds. For a time he was President of the Governor's Council, but, more important, became agent and receiver for the quit rents due Thomas, Lord Fairfax, for the Northern Neck, those enviable lands lying between the Potomac and the Rappahannock rivers. Tobacco, ever demanding virgin soil, paid for the "King's" long-vanished mansion, Corotoman, and for Christ Church, the serene chapel near which he was buried. Its doorway was patently prompted by one of the plates in William Salmon's *Palladio Londiniensis*, one of the British builders' guides that a planter might ponder on a long evening.

"The wretched, the widowed and the orphans, bereaved of their comforter, protector and father, alike lament his loss," ran the inscription on "King" Carter's tombstone. Which did not prevent an irreverent hand from scribbling these lines in chalk on the grave:

Here lies Robin, but not Robin Hood
Here lies Robin that never was good
Here lies Robin that God has forsaken
Here lies Robin the Devil has taken.

In the eighteenth-century civilization of Virginia a planter the like of "King" Carter was safe from the levelling influence of a town. He could send his tobacco off to London from a dock on his own lawn, and his chief worry might be the behavior of the factor in England supposed to provide the goods he ordered. A factor who misbehaved might be brought to account, as a certain William Hawkins learned on opening this letter from the "King."

"Now pray, upon the whole, where was your prudence, or rather, manners, to use with me the language that was hardly fit for your footman, if you keep one?" Carter made plain to Hawkins. "You might remember that I was your master's equal and all along have lived in as good rank and fashion as he did, even when you were something like Graves's cabin boy, and am old enough to be your father, not to mention any more reasons that justly give me a title to your deference. I shall conclude with telling you that I resolved to live in a calm, quiet air the rest of my days, and will be treated with respect by those who do my business. If you are so overgrown and tumefied with the little success you have had in the world, I would have you vent your vanities upon those that are to be gainers by you, and not upon your humble servant."

"King" Carter was not celebrated for his humility. Neither was his grandson Carter Burwell, who in 1751 began building Carter's Grove near Williamsburg, a grandiloquent tribute from Virginia to the grandeur of Sir Christopher Wren. Although the plan was conventional, with the great hall opening into four rooms, the latter two coupled with antechambers, the panelling of the two rooms on the first floor facing the James was something which even a supercilious Englishman might have approved, and the brickwork laid by the mason David Minitree showed that a planter building without benefit of an architect could set a standard.

Nothing so glorious was attempted by the Charles Carter who rebuilt Shirley in 1769. A square block of four rooms to a floor, dignified by twin two-story Palladian porticoes, its interest is more sentimental than historical: here was born the mother of Robert E. Lee.

A greater advertisement of the Carter style was Rosewell, Mann Page's mansion on the York River. Having taken a Carter for a wife, he went ahead in 1726 with a three-story brick palace. This was intended to be the most magnificent seat in the colony, and even in its ruinous condition is far from modest. The Episcopal Bishop William Meade, who had the manner of a Methodist and the moral fervor of a Presbyterian, was disgusted by this pile when he came to chronicle the families of Virginia in 1861. "We do not admit," he argued, "that anyone has the right thus to misspend the talent given him by God to be used for His Glory, and God often punishes such misconduct by sending poverty on the persons thus acting, and on their posterity."

Bishop Meade was also displeased by the prose of William Byrd II, who brightened the banks of the James with Westover in 1730. "The fault of his works," the Bishop indicated, "is an abundance of humor and of jesting with serious things, which sometimes degenerates into the kind of wit which so disfigures and injures the writings of Shakespeare."

Byrd was the grandson of a goldsmith in London, but his father had risen to be President of the Governor's Council and he himself studied law at the Middle Temple and made a friend of Sir Robert Walpole. Back in America William Byrd II laid his hands on 186,000 acres, incidentally amassing a handsome architectural library that included Colin Campbell's *Vitruvius Britannicus*. But he may have been fonder of the handbook of William Salmon than any other architectural item, at least the doorways of Westover were inspired by *Palladio Londinensis*.

Toward his agents in London he was as unforgiving as "King" Carter. "You will please to employ your interest with the tradesmen," he directed his factor, "not to send all the refuse of their shops to Virginia. Desire them to keep them for the customers that never pay them. 'Tis hard we must take all the worst of their people and the worst of their goods, too. But now shopkeepers have left off their bands, and their frugality, and their spouses must be maintained in splendor, 'tis very fit the sweat of our brows should help support them in it. Luxury is bad enough amongst people of quality, but when it gets amongst that order of men that stand behind counters, they must turn cheats and pickpockets to get it, and then the Lord have mercy on those who are obliged to trust to their honesty."

There were days when he dreamed of disposing of Westover and trading it for something similar in brick in England, and he hoped for a time when the Beckfords of Jamaica would take his place on the James. "If the torrid zone be still your choice, and you should resolve to lay your bones where you first drew your breath, be so good as to honor this country with one of your sons," he wrote Peter Beckford, grandfather of the William Beckford who would one day build an astonishing Gothic castle in Wiltshire back in England. "You may make a prince of him for less money here than you can make him a private gentleman in England."

There were other days when he was reconciled to his situation. "We that are banished from those polite pleasures," he told an English friend, "are forced to take up with rural entertainments. A library, a garden, a grove and a purling stream are the innocent scenes that divert our leisure." And he informed his old acquaintance the Earl of Orrery: "My Lord, we are very happy in our Canaan, if we could but forget the onions and fleshpots of Egypt. . . . We sit securely under our vines and our fig trees without any danger to our property. We have neither public robbers nor private, which your lordship will think very strange, when we have often needy governors and pilfering convicts sent amongst us."

Byrd admitted there were too many convicts in Virginia, but at least the people around him could put in a good day's work. This could not be said of the colony to the south. "To speak the truth," he maintained, " 'tis a thorough aversion to labor that makes people file off to North Carolina, where plenty and a warm sun confirm them in their disposition to laziness for their whole lives. The men . . . impose all the work upon the poor women. They make their wives rise out of their beds early in the morning, at the same time that they lie and snore till the sun has run one third of his course, and dispersed all the unwholesome damps. Then, after stretching and yawning for half an hour, they light their pipes, and under the protection of a cloud of smoke, venture out into the open air; though, if it happens to be never so cold, they quickly return shivering into the chimney corner."

Byrd could not believe that anyone in North Carolina would ever build a mansion as ambitious as Westover, and in his lifetime no one did. But in 1767 William Tryon, lately of Norbury Park, Surrey, having picked an heiress with 30,000 pounds for his wife, found himself Governor of North Carolina and could not resist proving to his subjects that he knew something about the art of living. By 1771, when he was promoted to be Governor of New York, he was the master at New Bern of what was locally regarded as a palace. Its architect was a certain John Hawks from Lincolnshire. Recently he had been earning his living as collector of the port at Beaufort, North Carolina, but had obviously been skimming builders' guides and architectural manuals in his evenings. One of his favorite books must have been Robert Morris's *Select Architecture*, where he could have come across in Plate X something very like the elevation of Tryon's Palace. Another building that may have had its influence on Hawks was Nuneham, the seat of the Earl of Harcourt in Oxfordshire, where two stairs, grouped in the middle, may have inspired the plan.

On the night of February 27, 1798, the palace went up in flames, but Hawks's elevation and plans were eventually deposited in the manuscript collection of the New-York Historical Society. Based on these records, work was begun in 1952 on the project intended to restore Hawks's achievement to something resembling its eighteenth-century dignity.

No such disaster befell Westover, although the Byrd family had its difficult moments before the century ended. William III, the son of William II, who married Mary Willing of Philadelphia—nicknamed "Willing Molly" by her enemies—on the death of his first wife Elizabeth Carter of Shirley, was a gambler. He played for the highest stakes, and lost. In 1777 he killed himself and it was his widow who welcomed

the Marquis de Chastellux, who pronounced this estate the most magnificent of all he inspected.

Nathaniel Harrison maintained the Byrd tradition of elegance at Brandon on the James, which he remodeled toward 1765 perhaps with the advice of his friend Thomas Jefferson. At least the charm of the central unit, two stories high, recalling a plate from Robert Morris's *Select Architecture*, deserves such an attribution, and the one-story wings are not disappointing.

Like the Byrds, the Lees of Stratford had their misadventures, which could hardly have been anticipated when Thomas Lee established his domain on the Northern Neck toward 1725. This Lee was an omnipotent real estate speculator, whose rise rivalled that of John Jacob Astor a century later. Before his death in 1750 he founded the Ohio Company, chartered with 500,000 acres in the west.

The H-plan of Stratford is unusual. So is the cunning contrivance of the doorways, obliging breezes to pass through the mansion on the most intolerable afternoons. But the distinguishing feature of Stratford is its rooftop whose arrogance almost recalls that of Sir John Vanbrugh's Kings Weston in Gloucestershire.

We may never know how the design of Stratford was conceived; not even the name of a mason has survived. But there is no doubt that Thomas Lee was an independent man, and it is hardly surprising that four of the six sons that Hannah Ludwell bore him did their best to upset the equilibrium of the British Empire. There was William, ostensibly a law-abiding businessman in London, but actually a sponsor of the arch-radical John Wilkes. There was Francis Lightfoot, signer of the Declaration of Independence. There was Arthur, an accomplice of Boston's rabble-rouser Sam Adams. And then there was Richard Henry, who found so much to admire in Patrick Henry.

The first shadow fell on Stratford after Matilda, niece of the Lees just mentioned, inherited the estate and married her cousin Henry Lee, "Light-Horse Harry." Famous for his gallant career with Washington's armies in the South, he made a competent Governor after playing a part in the state's adoption of the Constitution, and will always be remembered for the eulogy he gave of Washington—"first in war, first in peace, and first in the hearts of his countrymen." But although he had an inclination for rhetoric, he had none for business, and spent over two years in a debtors' prison when his land speculations went awry. Later he was to be brutally beaten in a Baltimore riot he tried to subdue. In 1818 he died a broken man.

"Black-Horse Harry," his son by Matilda, had an even sadder life. He was the guardian of his wife's sister, whose assets he dissipated, and so Stratford passed into her hands. This was not all. "He seduced her under circumstances too—too horrible to mention and blackened with his disgrace everyone that bore his name," claimed the conscientious judge Samuel Appleton Storrow. "Black-Horse" did succeed in winning an appointment as Consul General to Algiers, only to be rejected by the Senate. His last days were spent in exile in Paris. What this tragedy spelled to his half-brother Robert E. Lee, born at Stratford in 1807 to Ann Hill Carter, the second wife of "Light-Horse Harry," may be imagined.

In the neighborhood of Stratford is Mount Airy, built toward 1758 by John Tayloe, the only Virginian of the day credited with a race track of his own. Philip Fithian, the Princeton-educated tutor in the family of the Carters of Nomini Hall, was more than impressed by the Tayloe style. "Here is an elegant seat!" he recorded in his diary, "finished curiously and ornamented with . . . rich pictures. In the dining-room, besides many other fine pieces, are twenty-four of the most celebrated among the English race horses, drawn masterly and set in elegant gilt frames." Had Fithian made a careful study of the Tayloe library, he might have come across a copy of James Gibbs's *Book of Architecture*, first published in London in 1728. Besides being the designer of Saint Martin-in-the-Fields and the Senate House at Cambridge, Gibbs was so thoughtful as to reproduce an elevation of a gentleman's house in Dorsetshire which was obviously the model for the dark brown sandstone residence of Tayloe.

Tayloe's daughter Elizabeth had the intelligence to marry Edward Lloyd IV—Edward the Patriot, as he came to be known—of Wye House near Easton on the eastern shore of Maryland. Here she must have felt at ease, for there was an orangery at Wye House, dating perhaps from 1779, which was an elegant souvenir of Sir William Chambers's orangery at Kew Gardens, erected some twenty years before this for the Dowager Princess of Wales.

The original mansion at Wye House was burned to the ground at some unspecified date, but the grandeur of the Lloyds, who flew the family colors of azure and gold from their barge on Chesapeake Bay, is easily evoked, not only by the orangery but by the graveyard whose aged tombs, with their all but indecipherable inscriptions, remind us of Lloyds who died as far back as the seventeenth century. The grandest of all are the baroque monuments to Edward IV and his Tayloe wife.

Frederick Douglass, escaping from slavery to the career that finally made him American minister to Haiti, looked back, as you might imagine, without regret to the days when he was the slave of the Lloyds. "There were," he wrote in his autobiography, "certain secluded and out-of-the-way places . . . seldom visited by a single ray of healthy public sentiment, where slavery, wrapt in its own congenial darkness, could and did develop all of its malign and shocking characteristics, where it could be indecent without shame, cruel without shuddering, and murderous without apprehension or fear of exposure for punishment." Just such a secluded, dark and out-of-the-way place was the home plantation of the Lloyd of his time. Yet he admitted that "I have nothing cruel or shocking to relate of my own personal experience while I remained on Colonel Lloyd's plantation."

He also testified that "the stately mansions of the dead Lloyds" filled all the Negroes with forebodings. "Superstition was rife among the slaves about this family burying-ground," he reported. "Strange sights had been seen there by some of the older slaves, and I was often compelled to hear stories of shrouded ghosts, riding on great black horses, and of balls of fire which had been seen to fly there at midnight."

George Washington, who began building his Mount Vernon toward 1773, or six years before the orangery at Wye went up, was a generous if meticulous host, offering a glass from his cellars to "my *particular* and intimate acquaintances, some of the most respectable foreigners," and "persons of some distinction who may be traveling through the country from north to south." Yet he was not a gentleman of taste on the order of a Tayloe or a Lloyd. The plan of Mount Vernon is too accidental to have been premeditated, and Jefferson's friend Latrobe, while admitting that the President's retreat was "extremely good and neat," pronounced it "by no means above what would be expected in a plain English country gentleman's house of £500 or £600 a year."

Washington was aware of the handbooks of Batty Langley, which he found most useful when it came to installing a Palladian window at Mount Vernon, and if he had been as anxious about architecture as he was about the future of the United States, could have learned much from the visits he made to nearby Gunston Hall, the residence of George Mason who, "after a smart fit of the gout," drew up the Virginia Bill of Rights in 1776. To Mason may be credited the inspiration for the first ten amendments to the Constitution, but his insight was more than legal. He had the prescience to call on William Buckland, a young carpenter newly arrived from England as an indentured servant, to improve the house he had begun in 1755. To Buckland are attributed the porches, one of which is in the Gothic taste, and the remarkable interiors, including the Chinese Chippendale room and the Palladian drawing-room.

Buckland could be exquisite. By 1770 he was in charge of the Annapolis town house of the attorney Matthias Hammond, proving that his hand was as sure with an exterior as with an interior. The model for the bull's eye windows he found in James Gibbs's Saint Martin-in-the-Fields. Quite possibly Edward Lloyd IV lived to regret that Buckland executed only the interiors of the Annapolis dwelling that he purchased from Judge Samuel Chase. George Mason's find did so well in the New World that he had his portrait painted by Charles Willson Peale with the plan and elevation of Hammond's house before him.

Buckland had set a standard that no proud Virginian could neglect, and when Washington's step-grandson George Washington Parke Custis set about remodeling Arlington House overlooking the National Capital in 1820, he turned to George Hadfield, brother of the Maria Cosway that Jefferson had found so sympathetic; the result was a Doric triumph that may have partly compensated for the disappointment that was Hadfield's for the brief time he labored on the Capitol in Washington. In this house Robert E. Lee was married to Custis's only child. Here Lee was living until the outbreak of the Civil War.

In the meantime John Hartwell Cocke, who had interfered so often with Jefferson's plans for the University of Virginia, made up his mind to play architect himself. His aim, he made plain in 1818 when he laid the cornerstone of Bremo near Charlottesville, was to dispense "hospitality without riot or ostentation." Was he, as his acquaintance Edmund Ruffin insisted, "benevolent and good, though extremely narrow-minded"? A recognized authority on calcareous manures, Ruffin was a difficult man himself, so extravagant an apologist for slavery that he held

Jefferson had done incalculable harm by drafting the Declaration of Independence. He was also positive that Lord Byron should have brought *Don Juan* to an end with the eighth canto. "Then all would have been, however objectionable in regard to decency and morality, very interesting and showing great talent." For Poe he had less respect, judging that "whatever of genius or other talent, his strange writings may exhibit, they are as monstrous and abominable as his morals." It is only fair to add that holding these opinions did not prevent Ruffin from being idolized by Governor James Henry Hammond of South Carolina and other right-wing intellectuals promoting secession. Ruffin was granted the honor of firing the first shot on Fort Sumter. Whether he lived to regret this distinction is doubtful, although he took his own life in the summer of 1865.

Ruffin's acquaintance Cocke did ask Jefferson's advice on Bremo. "Palladio is the Bible," he was told. Also recommended was the Doric order. In spite of this he preferred the Tuscan and went ahead with a flat roof, never heeding his neighbor's warning about the walls to support such a roof. When the roof leaked, Jefferson was blamed. In his diary Cocke complained: "Commenced taking off roof of the house to be replaced by a new one to get rid of the evils of flat roofing and spouts and gutters, or in other words to supersede the Jeffersonian by the common sense plan." Although other friends were called upon, and James Dinsmore and John Neilson, two of Jefferson's disciples, made the final working drawings besides contracting for the carpentry, Bremo must be considered the creation of Cocke himself. Wisely, he had the capitals carved by his able slave Cato.

Bremo is one of the greater mansions of the South. The magnificence of the rough stone barn is arresting, and the twin dependencies of the house, connected by balustraded walks, reveal a sure eye. Cocke the experimenter is also revealed in Bremo Recess, the small Gothic villa he built for himself while the mansion was under construction. Possibly he was harking back at the Recess to Bacon's Castle, the seventeenth century dwelling of Arthur Allen in Surry County. Certainly he was extending a Gothic invitation to his son Philip Saint George Cocke, one of the great patrons on the eve of the Civil War.

When Philip Saint George Cocke went about building Belmead, his seat in Powhatan County, he summoned Alexander Jackson Davis of New York, the protégé of Andrew Jackson Downing, the landscape architect busy instructing Americans in seductive prose that only the Gothic would do for the house of an ambitious man. Belmead, erected in 1845, may now be little more than a ruin, but it proves that a wise Southerner was not above paying attention to the last word from the North.

There were, of course, Virginians raging with resentment toward fashions imported from the North. One of these was Nathaniel Beverley Tucker, author of *The Partisan Leader*, a curious novel prophesying the war to come. "I thank God that the fashion has not yet reached us," exclaims one of Tucker's spokesmen. "A woman, exposed to notoriety, learns to bear and then to love it. When she gets to that, she should go North; write books, patronize abolition societies, or keep a boarding school. She is no longer fit to be the wife of a Virginia gentleman."

To Philip Saint George Cocke this sort of talk was nonsense. He was more than satisfied with the Gothic tower of Belmead, and as a member of the Board of Visitors of the Virginia Military Institute (he became President of the Board once the buildings were under way), insisted that Davis design the barracks, the mess hall and the officers' quarters in his inimitable Gothic. Cocke was, of course, worried by the cloud he noticed on the horizon. "There are not a few," he wrote Davis in the winter of 1849, "who look to the Institute as a West Point for the South in case of disunion—which God forbid, but which the fanaticism of the North threatens to bring about."

With every year that passed, Cocke grew more devoted to Davis. "If I was autocrat or even Emperor (like Louis-Napoléon in France)," he was writing the architect in the spring of 1859, "I should delight with your aid to build up the waste places, repair dilapidations . . . and beautify the goodly and glorious heritage of our Rip Van Winkle people. But recollecting that I am but a democratic unit, I must limit and control these flights of fancy."

In the summer of 1859 he was hoping that he might give Davis one more chance. "Well!" he wrote him, "I am truly glad to know that you will come and see our great White Sulphur Springs, and select a site and give us the plan of an Episcopal chapel for that place." This was an ideal opportunity, for Richard Singleton of South Carolina had built the White Sulphur into almost the American equivalent of Bath, and who could tell what clients would emerge from the 1700 members of the Billing, Wooing and

Cooing Society that Singleton had invented. "I know," Cocke went on, "that you cannot go to that place and become acquainted with so many of our first Southern people, as you must and will do there, without its leading to many happy artistic and social results for Virginia and the Great South."

Nothing came of the plans for the chapel, and by December Cocke was near desperation. "What think you of the state of the country since the Brown invasion?" he was asking Davis three months after the raid on Harpers Ferry. "We are beginning here to beat our plowshares into swords and our pruning hooks into spears in good earnest. Our legislators will appropriate a half million for arming the militia. We ought to appropriate a million, and no doubt will, should affairs wax warmer. If your Conservative Party at the North does not *put down* and *put out* the accursed and pestiferous abolition faction, they will speedily bring about a dissolution of our hitherto glorious union.

"We at the South," he added, "shall be able to defend ourselves against this insane crusade, and when we shall have turned it back upon the North, what will become of law under morals and religion amongst a people who can not restrain the vilest of their population? Our slaves are quiet—happy and contented—and can not be instigated to revolt. But your revolutionists at the North may first force upon us a dissolution of the union and then turn insurgents in your midst to the overthrow of all law and order in their own section. It may be well for every conservative man in the North to think of these things."

With Philip Saint George Cocke as his champion, it was no wonder that Davis was appreciated in the Upper South. In Louisa County, not far from Bremo, he was asked by the planter Richard O. Morris to design Hawkwood, one of his subtler villas in the Italian style. And in North Carolina he could scarcely be challenged. The commission for the Grecian capitol at Raleigh—perhaps, with apologies to Jefferson, the greatest of all our state capitols—had fallen into his hands and those of his partner Ithiel Town in 1831. Close at hand was his Italianate state hospital. In nearby Chapel Hill was the Grecian library of the University of North Carolina (today the Playmakers' Theater). In Davidson near Charlotte was the original building, since destroyed, of Davidson College. And in Greensboro was the small but resolute Italian villa he planned for Governor John Motley Morehead, who not only sponsored the state hospital but also the North Carolina Central Railroad ultimately incorporated into the Southern system.

Of course Davis did not stand alone in North Carolina. Richard Upjohn came down from New York to plan Trinity Church in Raleigh, and Thomas U. Walter, whose career was underwritten by Nicholas Biddle of the Bank of the United States, was responsible for Saint James in Wilmington. Then there were the designers who remain as yet anonymous, like the inventors of Philanthropic Hall and Eumenean Hall on the Davidson campus, which might easily have passed for gate lodges on some early nineteenth-century English estate. Also anonymous is the artist who created the Doric portico toward 1840 at Orton Plantation on Cape Fear River: this was a property that had belonged since 1725 to the descendants of Maurice Moore. Finally no one yet knows who built the Grecian mansion of Edward Belo at Winston-Salem, not too far away from the Moravian remains of the eighteenth century.

And Philip Saint George Cocke could not be counted the only important patron of the Upper South on the eve of the war. The Bruces of Virginia may not be neglected. When James Bruce died in 1837 he was worth $1,500,000, part of it accumulated by wise investments in land and tobacco, part of it deriving from a series of country stores serving the farmers. His oldest son James Coles Bruce, who after attending the Universities of North Carolina, Harvard and Virgina, became one of the largest slaveholders of the South, once complained that whites were the real victims of slavery, since it "cheated the planters with a semblance of wealth." His own wealth was real. It was made evident in Berry Hill, the more than imposing Greek Revival mansion he built in Halifax County in 1845. On his death in 1865 he noted that he "felt a grim satisfaction in leaving the world at that time, as he knew that nothing but ruin was in store for his class."

Ruin was not in store for the Bruces. Philip Alexander Bruce, the scholar to whom other scholars will always be indebted for his exploration of the sources of seventeenth century Virginia history, had not yet published his first volume at the time. As for his brother William Cabell Bruce, his election to the United States Senate from Maryland lay far in the future, as did his biography of his fellow Virginian John Randolph of Roanoke. In our time William Cabell's son David K. E. Bruce, whose first wife was the daughter of Andrew Mellon, served as our Ambassador to France, England and Germany, completing his diplomatic career as United States Liaison Officer to the People's Republic of China.

These three Bruces were the descendants of Charles Bruce, half-brother of the master of Berry Hill, who relied on the talent of the West Point graduate John Johnston to create Staunton Hill, his admirable Gothic mansion in Charlotte County in 1848. We are told that when Charles Bruce died in 1896, "the only survivor of his class in that community, there was a universal feeling that the last representative there of the great slaveholding and landholding class was gone. One of his neighbors, a man in humble circumstances, rode many miles to attend his funeral, saying that he had come to see the burial of the last gentleman in the country. That funeral was one which for impressive simplicity has rarely been surpassed. There was no long train of carriages, as in a city, no lengthy procession of indifferent and conventional mourners. Borne in his coffin from his chamber to the library, the services were here held; then the coffin was lifted up by eight of his former slaves and carried through the grounds to the family graveyard followed, first by his children, then by his neighbors, and finally by a long line of laborers and their families."

Few Virginians were so fortunate as Charles Bruce. "I would not advise you to revisit Virginia at this time," William Pope Dabney, an old friend of Philip Saint George Cocke, wrote A. J. Davis in the spring of 1871. "The old hereditary mansions are in the hands, not of owners—for nobody is able to buy —but of the old overseer class, who rent them from the assignees in bankruptcy, and work a small patch themselves, and with their sons. The old planter is gone. The slaves are living in huts in the pines, eking out a miserable half-starving condition by petty thefts and depredations. We did have a hope that Northern thrift and capital would come along and buy up these deserted farms, but, misrepresented by the carpet-baggers who hold all our offices, and lie upon us in Congress, unfriendly legislation is driving capital and labor from all our borders. Our people would recognize the *logic of events*, and would welcome the rule of the old flag, but the refusal of amnesty has converted every man of any position before the war into an enemy of the government, and you can imagine what this will do."

Dabney could not forget Philip Saint George Cocke. After fighting at First Manassas, Cocke rose to be Brigadier General of the Northern Department of the State, only to be demoted. Resigning from the army, he returned to Belmead, where he committed suicide on the day after Christmas, 1861. "I spent the day before with him, and never saw him more rational," Dabney told Davis. Cocke himself wrote of his demotion: "I think General Lee has treated me very badly, and I shall never forgive him for it."

Lee, who had nothing to do with Cocke's demotion, harbored no grudges. In the spring of 1866 he stole a moment from his labors as President of Washington Academy at Lexington (the Washington and Lee University of the future) to write to Mrs. Charles P. Chouteau of Saint Louis, whom he had known on his tour of duty there nearly thirty years before. He was happy to send her his autograph. "I also enclose the last photograph of me," he added. "I have nine taken in uniform—but they are all alike and tempt me almost to deny myself. Do you recognize your old Uncle? You will ever live in my memory as my *beautiful Julie,* and I require nothing to recall you to my recollection. You stand before me now as you then appeared, in the vivid sunlight of youth and joy; undimmed by a single shadow of the intervening years. . . . I am," he closed, "considered such a reprobate that I hesitate to darken the doors of those whom I regard, lest I should bring upon them some dislike. But I hope some day that I may again see you, so that your little children may not learn to abhor me."

Maison Carrée, Nîmes, 16 B.C (architect unknown).

Capitol, Richmond, Virginia (Thomas Jefferson).

Hôtel de Salm (Palace of the Legion of Honor), Paris, 1782–87 (Pierre Rousseau). Open.

Château de Bagatelle, Paris, 1777–89 (François-Joseph Bélanger). Open.

La Maison du Désert, Chambourcy, 1772 (François Barbier).

Pavillon de Madame du Barry, Louveciennes, 1771 (Claude-Nicolas Ledoux).

Barrière du Trône, Paris, 1785–89 (Claude-Nicolas Ledoux). This was one of the many toll-houses that confronted Jefferson.

Gothic Temple, Pain's Hill, c. 1750 (Batty Langley) .

Temple of the British Worthies, Stowe, 1733 (William Kent). Open.

Chiswick, London, 1725-29 (The Earl of Burlington and William Kent).
Open.

Villa Rotunda, Vicenza, 1552–91 (Andrea Palladio and Vincenzio Scamozzi). Exterior Open.

Monticello, Residence of Thomas Jefferson. Charlottesville, Virginia, 1770–1809 (Thomas Jefferson). Open, Thomas Jefferson Memorial Foundation.

Poplar Forest, Residence of Thomas Jefferson, Lynchburg, Virginia, 1806–09 (Thomas Jefferson).

Pavilion III, University of Virginia, Charlottesville, Virginia, c. 1817
(Thomas Jefferson).

Pavilion IX, University of Virginia, Charlottesville, Virginia, c. 1817
(Thomas Jefferson.)

Rotunda, University of Virginia, Charlottesville, Virginia, 1822–26. (Thomas Jefferson).

Serpentine Walls, University of Virginia, Charlottesville, Virginia, c. 1817 (Thomas Jefferson).

Christ Church, Lancaster County, Virginia, 1732 (architect unknown).

Carter's Grove, Residence of Carter Burwell, James City County, Virginia, c. 1751–53. Front hall and exterior (architect unknown). Open, Colonial Williamsburg.

Shirley, Residence of Charles Carter, Charles City County, Virginia, c. 1769. (architect unknown). Open, Mr. & Mrs. Charles Hill Carter, Jr.

Ruins of Rosewell, Residence of Mann Page, Gloucester County, Virginia, c. 1726 (architect unknown).

Westover, Residence of William Byrd II, Charles City County, Virginia, c. 1730 (architect unknown). Private. Grounds and gardens open.

Tryon's Palace, New Bern, North Carolina, 1767–70 (John Hawks). Open, Tryon's Palace Commission.

Brandon, Residence of Benjamin Harrison, Prince George County, Virginia,
c. 1765 (architect unknown). Gardens only open.

Stratford, Residence of Thomas Lee, Westmoreland County. Virginia, c. 1725 (architect unknown). Open, Robert E. Lee Memorial Foundation.

Mount Airy, Residence of John Tayloe, Richmond County, Virginia, c. 1758 (architect unknown).

Orangery, Wye House, Residence of Edward Lloyd IV, Easton, Maryland, c. 1781 (architect unknown).

The Tombs of the Lloyds, Wye House, Easton, Maryland.

Mount Vernon, Residence of George Washington, Mount Vernon, Virginia, 1759–87 (architect unknown). Exterior and Palladian Window. Open, Mount Vernon Ladies' Association.

Gunston Hall, Residence of George Mason, Lorton, Virginia, 1755 (William Buckland). Porch and Interior Doorway. Open, Society of Colonial Dames.

Residence of Matthias Hammond, Annapolis, Maryland, 1770–74 (William Buckland). Exterior and Dining Room. Open, Hammond-Harwood House Association.

Arlington, Residence of G. W. P. Custis, Arlington, Virginia, 1820 (George
Hadfield). *Open, National Park Service.*

Bremo, Residence of John Hartwell Cocke, Fluvanna County, Virginia, c. 1818 (John Hartwell Cocke). Exterior and stables.

Bremo Recess, Residence of John Hartwell Cocke, Fluvanna County, Virginia, 1815–19 (John Hartwell Cocke).

Bacon's Castle, Surry County, Virginia, 1650–76 (architect unknown). Originally built for one Arthur Allen, Bacon's Castle is named after Nathaniel Bacon, Jr., the planter who led the rebellion of 1676 against the royal governor Sir William Berkeley. Bacon never lived here, but the house was seized by three of his followers.

Belmead, Residence of General Philip Saint George Cocke, Powhatan County, Virginia, 1845 (Alexander Jackson Davis).

Barracks, Virginia Military Institute, Lexington, Virginia, 1851 (Alexander Jackson Davis).

House of the Commandant, Virginia Military Institute, Lexington, Virginia, 1851 (Alexander Jackson Davis).

*Hawkwood, Residence of R. O. Morris, Louisa County, Virginia, 1851
(Alexander Jackson Davis).*

Capitol, Raleigh, North Carolina, 1831–33 (Town & Davis). The clerk of the works was one David Paton.

Old Library, in 1979 the Playmakers' Theater, University of North Carolina, Chapel Hill, North Carolina, 1850. (Alexander Jackson Davis).

*Residence of John Motley Morehead, Greensboro, North Carolina, 1850,
(Alexander Jackson Davis). Open, John Motley Morehead Memorial Commission.*

Saint James Church, Wilmington, North Carolina, 1839 (Thomas U. Walter).

Portico, Orton Plantation, Orton, North Carolina, 1840 (architect unknown). Grounds open.

Residence of Edward Belo, Winston Salem, North Carolina, 1849 (architect unknown).

Berry Hill, Residence of James Coles Bruce, Halifax County, Virginia, 1845 (architect unknown). Mansion and Gate Lodge.

Staunton Hill, Residence of Charles Bruce, Charlotte County, Virginia, 1848 (John Johnston).

Washington College, in 1979 Washington & Lee University, Lexington, Virginia, 1824 (J. Jordan).

THE LOWER SOUTH

"I do not love to do business for a man who takes no care of his own affairs," declared Henry Laurens. One of the biggest businessmen of eighteenth-century Charleston, he despised gentility and had no use for the naive investor. "Such a one can never be a proper judge of the endeavors of his friends to serve him." The charm of Charleston in 1979 is manifest, but charm is suspect if facts are forgotten.

Although Mepkin, his plantation house, has vanished, Laurens brings to mind as does no one else the hard-headed speculators who provided the cash on which the architecture of South Carolina was based. The son of a saddler of Huguenot stock, he was the master not only of rice but of indigo plantations. And indigo, introduced by Eliza Lucas Pinckney from Antigua in 1744, was a staple whose importance matched that of cotton in the nineteenth century. Rejoicing in the bounty offered by the British government, South Carolinians were exporting over a million pounds annually before the Revolution.

But Laurens was more than a planter. Dealing in everything from marble mantels and deerskins to rum and claret, he and his agents were respected in Lisbon and Madrid, in London and Glasgow, in every trading post of consequence in the West Indies, as well as in Boston, Philadelphia and New York. And by the eve of the Revolution he was also active in La Rochelle, Nantes and Bordeaux. Nor did he neglect the Guinea trade, on which he managed to make ten per cent profit.

He was annoyed when Egerton Leigh, a Charlestonian who devoted part of his income to collecting old masters, claimed he abandoned the slave trade from "goodness of heart." This, he protested, was a falsehood. But in 1768 he explained himself. "If you knew the whole affair," he told a friend, "it would make your humanity shudder. I have been largely concerned in the African trade. I quitted the profits arising from that gainful branch principally because of the many acts from the masters and others concerned toward the wretched Negroes, from the time of purchasing them to that of selling them again, some of which, within my knowledge, were uncontrollable." While he realized that slaves from Gambia proved amenable, he also understood that those from Calabar would commit suicide rather than endure captivity. There had been an insurrection near Charleston in the fall of 1739, foretelling Denmark Vesey's plot of 1822 and that of Nat Turner of 1831 in Virginia.

The most cultivated man in Laurens's world was Ralph Izard. Izard lived modestly in Charleston, but it must not be forgotten that he was the only American, apparently, to keep a town house in London. There he played upon the violin and the organ and rarely missed a concert by J. C. Bach, whom he found more accomplished than any of the musicians he heard in Rome. There is no doubt that he knew his way in the polite world. When he and his wife Alice De Lancey of the New York Tory family set off on their grand tour of the continent, they sat for Copley in Rome and their only real disappointment was missing Voltaire at Ferney. Their companion on that occasion was Arthur Lee of Stratford. "We were admitted no farther than his courtyard," Izard informed Laurens, "and upon sending in our names, the servant brought this answer: *Par dieu je suis malade.* We were taught to expect this, before we went. His age and infirmities made him peevish, and the intrusion of many stupid young traveling Englishmen, who have visited him, as strangers do lions, in the tower, has given him such a disinclination to company, that it is very difficult to get admittance to him."

With the American Revolution, Izard had to surrender his house on Berners Street. "It gives me," the Earl of Shelburne wrote him, "excessive concern when I hear of an American of your property and character quitting this country. I cannot persuade myself, yet, that our infatuation is irrecoverable, and that things may not still return to our old and natural union.'"

Benjamin Franklin, told once too often by Izard that nothing was to be gained by running around with men of no social position like the *Philosophes* of Paris, may have wished that the gentleman from South Carolina had never attempted to enter the diplomatic corps. But Izard would serve his country, even though "the anxiety of his mind . . . brought on a dreadful fit of the gout, which threatened his life and confined him in a state of helplessness for several months to his bed." The post that he coveted was that of Commissioner to the court of Tuscany in Florence. When the Grand Duke declined to receive him, he stayed on in Paris to Franklin's alarm, and after our independence was achieved, determined to set Jefferson on the right track. "Our governments tend too much to democracy," he cautioned him. "A handicraftsman thinks an apprenticeship necessary to make him acquainted with his business. But our back countrymen are of opinion that a politician may be born as well as a poet."

Very likely Izard's knowledge of the Back Country was secondhand. This was fortunate, if we may trust the diary of Charles Woodmason, a frantic parson of the Church of England who, visiting Pine Tree Hill (the Camden of our times) in 1766, found "the people around of abandonned morals and profligate principles, rude, ignorant, void of manners, education or good breeding. No genteel or polite person among them."

Woodmason was happier in the Low Country. The July, 1753, issue of *The Gentleman's Magazine* of London carried this stanza of his to the architectural glories to be found in the neighborhood of Charleston:

What! tho' a second Carthage here we raise,
A late attempt, the work of modern days,
Here Drayton's seat and Middleton's is found,
Delightful villas! Be they long renown'd.
Swift fly the years when sciences retire,
From frigid climes to equinoctial fire:
When Raphael's tints and Titian's strokes shall faint
As Fair America shall deign to paint . . .
Domes, temples, bridges rise in distant views
And sumptuous palaces the sight amuse.

One temple that Woodmason must have visited was Saint James, Goose Creek, near Moncks Corner, where the hatchment of Izard (the panel bearing his arms) may be seen to this day. In fact, wherever one turned, one could not escape Izard's respectable influence on architecture, His son-in-law Gabriel Manigault would become an architect in his own right, and Miles Brewton, whose town house was the envy of Charleston, selected one of Izard's cousins for his wife. The church of Izardian pomp and circumstance was undoubtedly Saint Michael's, an admirably free recollection of Saint Martin-in-the-Fields begun in 1752 by a designer whose name has been lost.

John Drayton, who erected Woodmason's favorite country seat in 1738, was evidently richer than Izard. He was a rice planter who climbed into His Majesty's Council, no matter if gossip claimed that he stopped in one tavern too many in town. Like William Byrd II, this Drayton was happy to rely on Salmon's *Palladio Londiniensis* for the mantels of his mansion, the most magnificent of the colony.

A later John Drayton, the Governor of the State in 1800, fell into ecstasy on contemplating the prosperity that rice had introduced into the New World. "At an early period," he wrote in his *View of South Carolina*, "gentlemen of fortune were invited to form . . . happy retreats from noise and bustle. . . . Here elegant buildings arose, which overlooked grounds, where art and nature were happily combined. Gardeners were imported from Europe; and soon the stately laurel, and the soft spreading elm shot up their heads in avenues and walks. . . . And nature, drawn from her recesses, presented landscapes diversified and beautiful, where winds had not long before shook the trees of the forest, or savages had roamed, impatient of government and control."

The Draytons could not enjoy this idyllic existence for long. William Drayton II, who moved to Philadelphia before his death in 1846, was disgusted by the very mention of the word secession. Perhaps it was no wonder that his son Percival was declared "infamous" by the South Carolina legislature. Besides taking part in Commander S. F. du Pont's expedition against Port Royal in 1861, Percival also fought with Farragut at Mobile Bay. Opposing him, however, was his brother Brigadier General Thomas Fenwick Drayton, whose loyalty to the Confederacy was never in question. "He is a gentleman and a soldier in his own person, but seems to lack the capacity to command," Lee regretfully conceded to Jefferson Davis. His brigade was broken up.

Drayton Hall, today minus its two flankers a property of the National Trust, might have been set afire by Sherman's troops if a Confederate officer had not had the presence of mind to lodge in the mansion a number of Negroes suffering from smallpox. Nearby Middleton Place with its imposing gardens (said to have been the creation of Henry Middleton, who inherited the estate from his father-in-law John Williams) was not so lucky. Northern troops burned the left flanker and the three-story central block in 1865, leaving only the right flanker to remind us of the dignity of this family. Arthur Middleton, Henry's son, was one of the signers of the Declaration of Independence; Williams Middleton, Arthur's grandson, paid his respects to the Declaration by signing the Ordinance of Secession.

More curious but less important than Middleton Place is Mulberry Castle near Saint James, Goose Creek, designed in 1714 to please Thomas Broughton, a future governor of the colony. The pagoda-like roofs of the pavilions are singular, and so are the jenkin-head gables under the gambrel roof of the second story. To be technical for a moment, the splaying-off of the peak of a gable with a third plane was one of the tricks of the trade of Charleston carpenters.

The builders of South Carolina houses evidently had handbooks aplenty. There is an echo of Palladio in more than one of the frame dwellings of coastal Beaufort. One of the best of these is that of Eliza Hext, dating possibly from 1720. But the most distinguished house in Beaufort may be Marshlands, built by J. B. Verdier in 1814. Its colonnaded porch above a ground floor devoted to security from the local insects indicates an awareness of necessities not invariably discovered in the architecture of the South. However, there is no question that carpenters knew how to catch the trade winds in Charleston. Typical of the city are the long and narrow *single* houses whose gable ends face the street, and whose sides exhibit inviting piazzas.

The most ambitious surviving town house of Charleston is that of the merchant Miles Brewton, built in 1769 with the aid of the housewright Ezra Waite. It was too ambitious, according to John Adams's high-minded young friend Josiah Quincy, Jr., who descended on the city in 1773, charged with a moral fervor that would not condone extravagance. He was not the man to forgive the Middletons for sitting to Benjamin West, or Brewton himself for sitting to Sir Joshua Reynolds. Nor was he the man to praise Charleston for permitting in the year he arrived the opening of David Douglas's permanent theater.

Quincy made his presence known at a meeting of the Saint Cecilia Society, and also his misgivings. Ralph Izard often played with the orchestra of the society, and Quincy had to admit that "the music was good. The two bass viols and French horns were grand. One Abercrombie, a Frenchman . . . played a first fiddle and solo incomparably, better than any I

ever heard." But Abercrombie was paid five hundred guineas a year, a sum that called for reflection. As for the gentlemen, "many of them dressed with richness and elegance uncommon with us."

When it came to the services of the Church of England he attended, they were reprehensible. "A young, scarcely-bearded boy read the prayers," he reported, "with the most gay, indifferent and gallant air imaginable." Nor was Quincy pleased with the manners of the congregation. "It was very common in prayer-time as well as sermon-time to see gentlemen conversing together. In short, taking a view of all things, I could not help remarking . . . that here was not, certainly, *solemn mockery*."

When he went to dine at Brewton's he was in the presence of genuine luxury. Although he did not notice the Palladian window facing the garden (perhaps in homage to Saint Martin-in-the-Fields) and failed to admire Ezra Waite's brickwork, he had to confess that Brewton's wine was "by odds the richest I ever tasted: exceeds Mr. Hancock's, Vassall's, Phillips's and others much in flavor, softness and strength." And he allowed that his host had "the grandest hall I ever beheld." But what did it matter that here were "azure blue satin window curtains" and "excessive grand and costly looking-glasses"?

Politics started before dinner, and Quincy discovered that one of the guests was "a hot sensible flaming Tory."

The final judgment of this New Englander on Southern civilization was predictable. "State, magnificence and ostentation, the natural attendants of riches, are conspicuous among this people: the number and subjection of their slaves tend this way. Cards, dice, the bottle and horses engross prodigious portions of time and attention: the gentlemen (planters and merchants) are mostly men of the turf and gamesters. Political inquiries and philosophical disquisitions are too laborious for them: they have no great passion for to shine and blaze in the forum or a senate."

Worst of all, "the state of religion here is repugnant not only to the ordinances and institutions of Jesus Christ, but to every law of sound policy."

But when Miles Brewton and his Izard wife were lost at sea, there were other Charlestonians who chose to live in the grand manner. There was William Gibbes, whose graceful frame mansion was apparently completed in the year the Constitution was ratified. There was William Blacklock, whose discreet brick residence now serves as the clubhouse of the College of Charleston. Finally, there was Nathaniel Russell, who *may* have called upon Russell Warren of Rhode Island to create the simple but superb elegance in 1811 of his town house on Meeting Street.

All this meant cash on hand. Although Edward Rutledge, elected Governor of South Carolina, worried for long over the Declaration of Independence, fearing the "low cunning" of the New Englanders and the spread of "those levelling principles which men without character and without fortune in general possess," Charleston was so prosperous at the dawn of the nineteeth century as to afford an amateur architect of genuine distinction.

Like Charles Bulfinch in Boston, Gabriel Manigault began life with a more than comfortable income. Grandson of the Gabriel Manigault who died in 1781 one of the richest merchants of the time, he read law at Lincoln's Inn after completing his studies in Geneva. Then, having married Ralph Izard's daughter Margaret, he determined to be more than just another rice planter. He was haunted by the buildings he had observed as a legal student in London, and may have remembered Henry Holland's Brooks Club when he composed the Charleston branch of the Bank of the United States in 1802. Holland may also have been in the back of his mind when he designed the now vanished Orphan House and the best of all his works, the town house of his brother Joseph in 1797. This has not been over-restored by the Charleston Museum which has opened it to the public.

Manigault set the stage as only a wise amateur could for the professional architects to come. But for his example William Strickland of Philadelphia might not have been invited in 1828 to plan the endearing building of the College of Charleston, which was politely improved in 1850 by the wings added by the local architect E. B. White. In that very year White got the commission to design the steeple of Saint Philip's. This church had been begun in 1835 by John Hyde. Hyde hoped, and his hope was realized, that Saint Philip's might rival even Saint Michael's as an Anglican landmark.

This might be the moment to venture into the High Hills of the Santee, a part of the Back Country that called down so many jeremiads from the Reverend Charles Woodmason. "Many hundreds live in concubinage," he reported in 1767, "swopping their wives as cattle, and living in a state of nature, more irregularly than the Indians." Here, as everywhere in his travels, he was exposed to the taunts of Baptists and Presbyterians, whom he frequently suspected of being in league with the Romans. Yet this region could not be considered hopeless. In 1821 Dr. William Wallace Anderson, who had wandered down from Maryland and married the niece of Thomas Hooper of North Carolina, thus inheriting a plantation at Stateburg, began rebuilding the former Hooper home into Borough House, a Palladian vision in *pisé de terre* or rammed earth with a two-storied Ionic colonnade that attracted visitors as distinguished as the botanist Joel R. Poinsett who was buried in the churchyard of the Holy Cross nearby. This was a Gothic design of 1850 in *pisé de terre*, the work of Edward C. Jones of Charleston, recently brilliantly restored by Henry Boykin with the advice of Captain Richard K. Anderson on pisé construction. So charming a church was beyond Woodmason's dreams, who did not know that Mrs. Anderson's aunt Mary Heron Hooper would be painted by Copley in London.

Borough House and the Holy Cross testified that architecture could be discovered far from Charleston. So did the Church of the Cross at Bluffton not too many miles from Savannah, a Gothic fancy in the richest cypress contrived by E. B. White in 1850. This was quite as remarkable as Sheldon Church near Beaufort, whose ruins, dating from the middle of the eighteenth century, told of real ambition in brick.

So Robert Mills of Charleston, the first American to be trained for the architectural profession, did not come from a discouraging world. Encouraged by James Hoban, the Irishman who spent some time in Charleston before winning the competition for the White House, Mills was welcomed by Jefferson at Monticello, who sent him on to Bulfinch and Latrobe. Latrobe did have doubts about this pupil, sensing that he was too prudent to be one of the adventurers of the nineteenth century. In Latrobe's eyes he was "a wretched designer. He came to me too late to acquire principles of taste. He is a copyist and is fit for nothing else," he told another architect. "But he has also his merit. He is a very snug contriver of domestic contrivances and will make a good deal of money. He wants that professional respect which is the ruin of you and me, and therefore we shall go to the wall, while he will strut in the middle of the street."

Was Latrobe quite fair? There may be more to Mills than he suspected. There is a dignity to the Doric portico of Camden's Bethesda Presbyterian Church, dating from 1820, and to Camden's court house of 1826. And in Columbia he showed his sure if not daring hand in the town house of the merchant Ainsley Hall in 1818. Then there is the reassuring court house of Walterboro. In Charleston itself there is the First Baptist Church, Doric again, as is the Record or Fireproof Building of 1827, whose monumentality has been recently revealed by Albert Simons's sensitive restoration.

Besides launching the Greek Revival in the South, Mills was the friend of all internal improvements in South Carolina, preaching the benefits of canals, railroads and lighthouses in one pamphlet after another. His message as an architect was of course understood outside his own state. In Richmond in 1818 he provided Aaron Burr's attorney John Wickham with the town house in the regency manner that today is the Valentine Museum. Later came the Washington Monument in Washington, completed long after his death and lacking the colonnade at the base that he deemed essential. Possibly he was better satisfied with the Washington Monument in Baltimore's Mount Vernon Place.

Mills said of this commission: "The education I have received being altogether American and unmixed with European habits, I can safely present the design submitted as American." This was naive. So was his advice to the younger men in the profession. "I say to our artists," he proclaimed, "study your country's tastes and requirements, and make classical ground *here* for your art. Go not to the old world for your examples. We have entered a new era in the history of the world; it is our destiny to lead, not to be led. Our vast country is before us and our motto *excelsior*."

There were South Carolinians of greater sophistication. In fact the most rewarding of all American artists in the early nineteenth century was Washington Allston, who sold the plantation he inherited near Georgetown to study with Benjamin West in England, where he became the intimate friend of Coleridge. If Allston required grandeur as a boy, he could have gazed at Hampton, the property of Daniel Huger Horry at McClellanville, whose Doric colonnade of pine may date from 1790. Neither grandeur nor sophistication may be claimed for the benevolent cotton mill magnate William Gregg, but he did have

the independence toward 1848 to build a mill town in the Gothic for his employees at Graniteville near Aiken.

At Aiken we are near the border of Georgia, which was raising three times as much Sea Island cotton as South Carolina before the Civil War. This may have been one of the reasons why the English architect William Jay moved to Savannah in 1817. His father, a dissenting preacher, was sorry that he had "a large share of wit and humor, qualities always dangerous and commonly injurious to the possessor. His comic powers drew him into company not the most friendly to youthful improvement." Despite this he was responsible for a Gothic villa that has disappeared from Sullivan's Island near Charleston, as well as three unforgettable residences for Savannah in the Regency manner. One of these, the so-called "Owens" house was for Richard Richardson, whose wife was Jay's sister-in-law. Another was for the merchant William Scarborough, and still another was planned for Alexander Telfair, son of Governor Telfair. The most distinguished of the three, this is today the Telfair Academy.

But the most extraordinary residence in Savannah on the eve of the war was that of the English merchant Charles Green, grandfather of the novelist Julien Green. "I was humiliated by this simple dwelling," commented Julien Green on seeing Savannah after living all his life in Paris. "But when I drew near, I changed my mind. It is well proportioned, and not without a certain grandeur." It is fortunate that the novelist came to recognize the quality of this work of 1856 by the New York architect John S. Norris. Its Gothic dignity was appreciated in Civil War times by the British journalist William Howard Russell. "Italian statuary graced the hall," Russell wrote in his diary. "Finely carved tables and furniture, stained glass and pictures from Europe set forth the sitting-room, and the luxury of bathrooms and a supply of cold fresh water rendered it an exception to the general run of southern offices." This was the house that was handed over to General Sherman when he offered the city as a Christmas present to Lincoln at the end of his march to the sea.

Russell was far from complimentary to the Southerners he met at Morris Island at the time of the attack on Fort Sumter. "These tall, thin, fine-faced Carolinians are great materialists," he claimed. "The worshippers here are not less prostrate before the *almighty dollar* than the Northerners. . . ." "*Tom is a little cut, sir, but he is a splendid fellow, he's worth half a million of dollars,*" one soldier was saying of another. "This reference to a money standard of value was not unusual or perhaps unnatural, but it was made repeatedly; and I was told wonderful tales of the riches of men who were lounging around, dressed as privates, some of whom were at that season, in years gone by, looked for at the watering places as the great lions of American fashion. But secession is the fashion here. Young ladies sing for it; old ladies pray for it; young men are dying for it; old men are ready to demonstrate it. . . . The utter contempt and loathing for the venerated stars and stripes, the abhorrence of the very words United States, the intense hatred of the Yankee on the part of these people, cannot be conceived by anyone who has not seen them. I am more satisfied than ever that the Union can never be restored as it was, and that it has gone to pieces, never to be put together again, in the old shape, at all events, by any power on earth."

If Russell had been a more conscientious reporter, he would have admitted that the hysteria was not unanimous. "Where's the fire?" asked the respected attorney James L. Petitgru of a fellow South Carolinian. "Mr. Petitgru, there is no fire," he was told. "These are the joybells ringing in honor of the passage of the Ordinance of Secession." "I tell you there is a fire," Petitgru claimed. "They have this day set a blazing torch to the temple of constitutional liberty, and, please God, we shall have no more peace forever."

Nor was Benjamin Franklin Perry, the former editor of the Greenville *Mountaineer*, enraptured by disunion. "Judging from the course pursued by other Presidents," he wrote in the summer of 1860, "it is likely Lincoln will pursue a very cautious, politic and wise course toward the South." When secession was sure, Perry was embarrassed. "I have been trying," he said, "for the last thirty years to save the state from the horrors of disunion. They are now going to the devil and I will go with them."

"One great cause of our failure," Perry wrote when it was all over, "was that the heart of the Southern people was never in this revolution! There was not a state, except South Carolina, in which there was a majority in favor of secession!"

Residence of Ralph Izard, Charleston, South Carolina, c. 1757 (architect unknown).

Saint James, Goose Creek, South Carolina, c. 1711 (architect unknown). Exterior and interior.

Saint Michael's Church, Charleston, South Carolina, 1752–56 (architect unknown).

Drayton Hall, Residence of John Drayton, near Charleston, South Carolina,
c. 1738 (architect unknown). Exterior and Mantel. Open, National Trust.

Flanker of Middleton Place, Residence of John Williams, near Charleston, South Carolina, c. 1735 (architect unknown). Grounds open.

Mulberry Castle, Residence of Thomas Broughton, near Charleston, South Carolina, c. 1714 (architect unknown).

Residence of Eliza Hext, Beaufort, South Carolina, c. 1720 (architect unknown).

*Marshlands, Residence of J. R. Verdier, Beaufort, South Carolina, c. 1814
(architect unknown).*

Residence of Miles Brewton, Charleston, South Carolina, c. 1769 (architect unknown). Exterior and Drawing Room.

Residence of John Stuart, Charleston, South Carolina, c. 1772 (architect unknown). This is a typical example of the Charleston "single house."

Residence of William Gibbes, Charleston, South Carolina, c. 1789 (architect unknown).

Residence of Nathaniel Russell, Charleston, South Carolina, c. 1811 (architect unknown). Open, Historic Charleston Foundation. Exterior and Drawing Room (facing).

Residence of William Blacklock, Charleston, South Carolina, c. 1800 (architect unknown). Serving in 1979 as the faculty club of the College of Charleston.

Bank of the United States, Charleston, South Carolina, 1802 (Gabriel Manigault).

Residence of Joseph Manigault, Charleston, South Carolina, 1797 (Gabriel Manigault). Open, Charleston Museum. Gate Lodge, Exterior and Dining Room.

Orphan House, Charleston, South Carolina, 1802 (Gabriel Manigault). Destroyed.

College of Charleston, Charleston, South Carolina, 1828 (William Strick-land).

Saint Philip's Church, Charleston, South Carolina, 1835–38 (Joseph Hyde).
The steeple was added in 1850 by E. B. White. On the left may be seen the
restoration of the Dock Street Theater that opened in 1736 with Farquhar's
The Recruiting Officer; *on the right, the Huguenot Church designed by*
E. B. White in 1844–45.

Church of the Holy Cross, Stateburg, South Carolina, 1850 (Edward C. Jones).

Borough House, Residence of Dr. William Wallace Anderson, Stateburg, South Carolina, c. 1821 (architect unknown). House and Doctor's Office. Private.

Church of the Cross, Bluffton, South Carolina, c. 1850 (E. B. White).

Ruins of Sheldon Church near Beaufort, South Carolina, 1745–47 (architect unknown).

Bethesda Presbyterian Church, Camden, South Carolina, 1820 (Robert Mills). Two views.

Court House, Camden, South Carolina, 1826 (Robert Mills). Four Greek Doric columns were substituted in 1847 for the original six sandstone Ionic columns of the portico.

Residence of Ainslee Hall, Columbia, South Carolina, 1818 (Robert Mills).
Open. Historic Columbia Foundation.

Court House, Walterboro, South Carolina, c. 1822 (Robert Mills). This was enlarged in 1939.

First Baptist Church, Charleston, South Carolina, c. 1820 (Robert Mills).

Fireproof Building, Charleston, South Carolina, 1822–27 (Robert Mills).

Residence of John Wickham, Richmond, Virginia, 1812 (Robert Mills).
Open, Valentine Museum.

Washington Monument, Baltimore, Maryland, 1809–29 (Robert Mills).

Hampton, Residence of Daniel Huger Horry, near Georgetown, South Carolina, c. 1735, Portico, c. 1790 (architect unknown).

Mill housing, Graniteville, South Carolina, c. 1848 (architect unknown).

Residence of Richard Richardson, Savannah, Georgia, 1817 (William Jay).
Open, Telfair Academy.

*Residence of William Scarborough, Savannah, Georgia, 1818 (William Jay).
Open, Historic Savannah Foundation.*

*Residence of Alexander Telfair, Savannah, Georgia, 1818 (William Jay).
Open, Telfair Academy.*

Residence of Charles Green, Savannah, Georgia, 1856 (John S. Norris).
Open, Saint John's Parish.

THE DEEP SOUTH

The trouble with Edna Pontellier, as you will remember if you have given a recent glance to Kate Chopin's New Orleans novel *The Awakening*, was that she was not a mother-woman. "It was easy to know them, fluttering about with extended, protecting wings, when any harm, real or imaginary, threatened their precious brood. They were women who idolized their children, worshiped their husbands, and esteemed it a holy privilege to efface themselves as individuals and grow wings as ministering angels." Perhaps it was no wonder that Edna cultivated her boredom with a particular quiet passion. She was indifferent to her husband's playing billiards at Klein's hotel on Grand Isle. She was also indifferent, if the truth be told, to Robert Lebrun and Alcée Arobin, who would flirt with her. So it was inevitable that, having cast her clothes on the shore, she sought her death by swimming out to sea.

Was *The Awakening* a *Southern* novel? Edna could easily have played the same role in a New York or Chicago suburb. A far more Southern production was the Connecticut Yankee John W. DeForest's *Miss Ravenel's Conversion from Secession to Loyalty*. "The people are dreadfully poky," says Miss Lillie Ravenel of New Orleans of the acquaintances she made in New Boston up north. "If you never lived with the Southerners you don't know how pleasant they are," Lillie claims. "There are low people everywhere. But I do say that the better classes of Louisiana and Mississippi and Georgia and South Carolina and Virginia, yes, and of Tennessee and Kentucky, are right nice. If they don't know all about chemistry and mineralogy, they can talk delightfully to ladies. I say that such people are civilized."

Miss Ravenel spoke with a certain authority. So did Harriet Beecher Stowe. Although Mrs. Stowe was never accused of being the champion of Southern civilization, she had nothing but pity in her heart for the mistresses of the Southern plantations when she came to write *Dred: A Tale of the Great Dismal Swamp*. "The duties of a Southern housekeeper, on a plantation, are onerous by any amount of Northern conception," she explained. "Every article wanted for daily consumption must be kept under lock and key, and doled out as need arises. For the most part, the servants are only grown-up children, without consid-

eration, forethought, or self-control, quarreling with each other, and divided into parties and factions, hopeless of any reasonable control. Every article of wear, for some hundreds of people, must be thought of, purchased, cut and made, under the direction of the mistress; and add to this the care of young children, whose childish mothers are totally unfit to govern or care for them, and we have some slight idea of what devolves on Southern housekeepers."

Mrs. Stowe does not seem to have suspected the degree of independence the Blacks might achieve once granted their emancipation, but she was, after her fashion, an honest chronicler—far more honest than recent popular historians of the Deep South who are fond of mentioning that beside every cup of coffee on a plantation breakfast tray would be found the inevitable magnolia blossom.

New Orleans, which counted over 100,000 inhabitants by 1840, was not only America's second port, but a city desperately dependent on cotton and sugar prices (by 1830 two thirds of America's sugar was supplied by Louisiana). Prices could fluctuate wildly: the inexorable laws of supply and demand prevailed here as elsewhere.

These laws were well understood by Vincent Nolte, a native of Leghorn who first saw New Orleans on Easter Sunday, 1806. Nolte was in need of no instruction on the curious course of the sugar and cotton markets. He was an intimate friend of Alexander Baring of the Baring Brothers of London, so intimate that this Baring dared ask him his opinion of the famous Hamburg financier David Parish. "Mr. Parish," Nolte replied, "shows more ability in getting out of scrapes than avoiding them." Nolte himself got into scrapes: in 1826 he went bankrupt when Hottinguer et Cie. in Paris declined to honor his notes. In later years Nolte could, if he liked, console himself by thinking of the fate of Nicholas Biddle of Philadelphia who, after bolstering the cotton market in the Panic of 1837 and taking up on his own a $5,000,000 loan to the State of Mississippi, vanished from the financial horizon when his Bank of the United States went under.

Nolte, who once dreamed of becoming a painter, and knew a thing or two about architecture (on visiting his father back in Hamburg he had come to know the distinguished French architect Ramée) might have been the perfect guide to the architecture of New Orleans in the early nineteenth century. But he is silent in his memoirs on this subject, perhaps because he was constantly troubled by the adventurers and worthless men from distant regions who tried to pass for honest men in the city.

Nolte must have paused when he passed by the Cathedral, the Presbytère and the Cabildo or government headquarters, whose singular charm told of the concern in Madrid for Louisiana before the province was returned to France to be surrendered to the United States. And when he stopped before the Blanc house on the Bayou Saint John whose graceful balcony proved there were wise artisans who obeyed the law of the climate, he may have congratulated himself for fighting at Jackson's side in the Battle of New Orleans. He could not have objected to the cast-iron balconies on Royal Street. But by the time James Gallier, Sr. laid out the Pontalba Apartments, he was back in Europe, reduced to surviving in Venice on bread, cheese and wine. He also missed seeing the imposing Corinthian town hall of Gallier, and the astute colonnades of the Robinson house of 1864 invented by Gallier's son.

Nolte's career reminds us of the exaltation and the anxiety of those who speculated on commodities in the Deep South. Native American investors also suffered, none more than the Hamptons of South Carolina, whose vicissitudes were typical of investors from the old South.

There was nothing quite like the land hunger of the Hamptons. Wade I, the founder of the dynasty, may be remembered as one of Thomas Sumter's generals in the Revolution. In his own time he was famous for the sharp eyes that sought out the richest acres. Nothing, not even the murder by raiding Cherokees of his father, his mother and his nephew, could check his advance in the world. A native of Halifax County, Virginia, he sized up South Carolina so accurately that by 1799 he was already marketing six hundred bales of cotton. What did it matter that he was denied even a common school education? Before he died in 1835 he was reckoned the wealthiest planter in the United States, and there were those who envied his participation in the Yazoo Fraud that opened up Alabama and Mississippi to four land companies for the modest sum of $500,000. He seems to have forecast the future of Louisiana, which his family was to find so attractive. But as early as 1796 Etienne de Boré

had proved that the local cane juice could yield crystalline sugar at a profit.

How well the Hamptons fared in Louisiana may be guessed by the $1,500,000 that changed hands in 1857 when the John S. Prestons (she was the sister of Wade II) disposed of one of their plantations, Houmas, with its respectable if not awe-inspiring Grecian house. The Prestons seem to have preferred living in Columbia, South Carolina, where they could exhibit the latest works of their protégé the sculptor Hiram Powers.

Like the Prestons, Wade II made his home in Columbia. Only the ruins are left of Millwood, his Greek Revival residence: it was set on fire by Sherman's troops when they came to occupy the city. A reporter for the *American Agriculturalist* in 1847 made much of Wade II's pure-bred Durham cattle and his choice flock of long-wooled sheep. More might have been made of the guests he entertained at Millwood. His education had evidently not stopped at South Carolina College, nor had his service in the War of 1812 narrowed his horizon, for he liked the company not only of Henry Clay and the historian George Bancroft, but also that of Dr. Samuel Gridley Howe. The day came when Dr. Howe's wife repaid the Hamptons for their hospitality by writing the words of *The Battle Hymn of the Republic*.

To the historian of the South Carolina Jockey Club Wade II was "the *embodied spirit* of Carolina blood and Carolina honor. No pilgrim," he added, "ever knelt at the shrine of My Lady at Loreto, nor dipped into the river Jordan with greater devotion" than he lavished on his stables. He did win the club's Tattersall whip for the performance of his imported colt Monarch.

Wade II died in 1858 $500,000 in debt. Despite his success at the race track, he had his burdens to bear. One of them was his brother-in-law James Henry Hammond, who managed to be elected Governor in 1842. The son of a schoolmaster from Massachusetts, Hammond grew almost too fond of the Peculiar Institution, especially after he married Mrs. Hampton's sister, the wealthy Catherine Fitzsimmons of Charleston. "Slavery is no evil," he announced. "On the contrary I believe it to be the greatest of all the great blessings which a kind providence has bestowed upon our glorious region." His biographer has told us that he could not "manifest his natural mildness to the slaves of his plantation near Augusta." In fact, "in order to bring them to their senses, he was compelled to be extremely severe for a year or more." He was equally severe on his white neighbors. When he showed off the collection of paintings and statuary he acquired during a grand tour of Europe, he made plain that they reacted "with the apathy of Indians." Whether he had any taste is debatable. Redcliffe, his plantation house at Beech Island near the Georgia line, is a pompous thing, although not completely uninspired, like the retreat of John C. Calhoun at Clemson. Hammond did have a certain talent for oratory. This he displayed in 1858 when he argued that "cotton is king. You dare not make war on cotton. No power on earth dares make war upon it."

Besides exulting in his oratorical skill, Hammond passed for a ladies' man. He was so indiscreet, Professor Clement Eaton revealed in *The Mind of the South*, as to seduce two of his wife's nieces, the daughters of Wade II. Wade II was discreet, sending word to Hammond's friends that unless they withdrew their candidate from the coming senatorial race, "an exposure would be made that would prostrate him forever." "Where was a statesman ever put down before for amorous and conjugal infidelity?" Hammond complained, but did find it prudent to move away from Columbia. The scandal does not seem to have done him any damage in the eyes of his close friend Edmund Ruffin, the Virginian who liked to lecture on "The Free Negro Nuisance and how to Abate It." Nor did it shock the local novelist William Gilmore Simms, whose own capacity for self-pity was unlimited.

Now that Millwood is nothing but a ruin, the best example of the Hampton way of life may be Milford Plantation in the sand hills of Clarendon County, not too far from Sumter, South Carolina. This, the most extravagant Greek Revival house in the state, was begun in 1839 by the Rhode Island architect Nathaniel F. Potter for Governor John Laurence Manning, who had the prescience to marry Susan Frances Hampton, the sister of Wade II. Although little enough is known about Potter's career, he was well-trained, having been associated in Providence with the firm of Talman and Bucklin, responsible for the Providence Arcade and other local landmarks. In South Carolina he had worked as a brick-mason on Charles F. Reichardt's Charleston Hotel, but was much more than a mason at Milford, whose elegance was so sure that it became immediately famous as Manning's Folly.

After the war Milford was to become rather like a castle in a German fairy tale. Although no stranger made his appearance, and there was no fountain in the forest, these stage properties were not missed. The tale was told that General Robert Brown Potter of the United States Army showed up in 1865 just in time to stop a Negro from shooting Governor Manning. This General Potter, the legend ran, was the son of Bishop Alonzo Potter of New York, and the brother of the architect. The fact is that this General Potter never saw service in South Carolina and was, apparently, no relation of Nathaniel. Possibly, quite possibly, General Edward E. Potter showed up at Milford, for he was conducting raids in the neighborhood. Was he a relation of the architect? This is doubtful.

The Deep South itself remains legendary, which is not surprising when one recalls that even investors as sharp as the Hamptons and Vincent Nolte had their misadventures. Not every plantation owner will be fully identified: this is what one must expect in the case of fortunes quickly gained and as quickly lost. But as we glance at the architecture from the tobacco fields of Kentucky down to the cotton and sugar plantations further South, it will become obvious that the South was following the Greek and Gothic fashions of the North, just as the South in the colonial era looked to England for inspiration. There will be extraordinary buildings, but not too many inventions that served the particular demands of the Southern climate.

Talent was evident in Kentucky. This might have surprised Vincent Nolte, who visited the state not long after its admission to the Union, and shrank from the early Kentucky custom of cutting long finger-nails into sickles, the better to gouge out the eyes of victims in the local brawls. Manners had apparently improved by 1850 when Alexander Jackson Davis designed Loudoun, the Gothic mansion in Lexington of Francis Key Hunt, son of a prosperous hemp manufacturer. This was so capricious and so successful that the local architect John McMurtry, who had supervised its construction, was asked two years later to build Ingelside, another advertisement of the Gothic manner for Henry Boone Ingels, who had the presence of mind to marry the daughter of the iron founder Joseph Bruen (Ingelside has vanished; Loudoun is now in the custody of the Department of Parks.) Not that the Greek Revival was neglected. Scholarship was demonstrated by Gideon

Shryock, who recalled the temple of Athena Polias at Priene in Iona when he planned the capitol, at Frankfort, in 1830. And James Harrison Dakin, a graduate of the Davis office in New York, also turned to Grecian precedent when he composed the Bank of Louisville eight years later.

Kentucky's forthright abolitionist Cassius Marcellus Clay, the artist with the bowie knife who served as Lincoln's minister to Russia, might have been expected to build a Gothic castle, but White Hall, his mansion near Richmond, was designed toward 1865 in a gaunt Italianate style by Thomas Lewinski. However, he felt at home under Lewinski's sixteen-foot ceilings: he stood six feet three inches and weighed 215 pounds. At home or away from home he was far from shy, as Samuel M. Brown of New Orleans discovered on knocking him down at an anti-slavery rally. One of Brown's ears was sliced off, one of his eyes was gouged out, and his skull was slit to the bone. Friends of Brown tried to bring Clay to justice. This was impossible, for he was defended by his cousin Henry. "If he had not stood his ground," Henry Clay told the jury, "he would have been unworthy of the name he bears." Later on Cassius Marcellus Clay was disappointed when a favorite nephew was insulted, unarmed. "I am astounded that you wouldn't be armed," said Uncle Cassius. A day or two later the nephew came across the man who had provoked him. Yanking out his bowie knife, he struck him first in the cavity of his left armpit, then got him on each side of the breast bone. In all he struck him nine times before he dropped dead. The nephew was fatally wounded, but Cassius Marcellus Clay was satisfied. "I couldn't have done better myself," he admitted. White Hall is today a state shrine.

In Tennessee the Greek Revival was omnipresent, which will not surprise you if you remember that the capitol in Nashville, begun in 1845, fell into the hands of William Strickland, the veteran who had planned Nicholas Biddle's Grecian Bank of the United States in Philadelphia. The capitol was Strickland's greatest achievement: its dignity is almost as profound as that of the masterpieces of Carl Friedrich Schinkel in the classic tradition in Prussia. The cupola of the capitol showed that Strickland had carefully studied the Choragic Monument to Lysicrates: long ago he had made use of this in the Philadelphia Merchants' Exchange. He could hardly leave domestic architecture alone, and to him has been attributed the Italianate mansion in Nashville of the lawyer Joseph Acklen—later the Ward-Belmont College for women—as well as Belle Meade, the austere plantation house nearby of William Giles Harding. Harding may have been born in a log cabin, but was an enterprising citizen, the first to ship his hay to New Orleans and one of the first to recognize the importance of railroads. He was one of the charter subscribers to the Nashville and Chattanooga Line. His reward was the deer park of four hundred acres he maintained on his four-thousand acre estate. Another planter who appreciated the Greek Revival was George Polk, brother of the fighting bishop Leonidas Polk, who built Rattle and Snap near Columbia. Still another in the Columbia neighborhood was Gideon Pillow, although he veered slightly to the Gothic in the pointed windows of the office of his property.

Like Tennessee, Alabama was Grecian territory. Mobile was distinguished by the Barton Academy and the Government Street Presbyterian Church by James Harrison Dakin and his brother Charles B. Dakin, while Florence further north was honored by the commanding Corinthian colonnade of James Jackson's Forks of Cypress, recently levelled by fire. By far the most ambitious house in the state was Gaineswood at Demopolis, the seat of General Nathan Bryan Whitfield. Only occasionally was the Gothic attempted: one example was the cottage at Opelika, dating perhaps from the fall of 1865, of John Calhoun Edwards, who seems to have read and pondered the advice of the Northern Gothic prophet Andrew Jackson Downing.

Although Windsor at Port Gibson may be the most spectacular Grecian ruin in the United States—this Corinthian paradise of the planter Smith C. Daniel went up in flames in 1890—Mississippi also endorsed the Gothic, as in Dr. Charles Bonner's house at Holly Springs, and even the Moorish. In fact the most unusual plantation house of the Deep South was Longwood at Natchez, begun in 1860 and never completed by Haller Nutt, whose father, a Virginian by birth, had studied medicine with Rush in Philadelphia and toured the Near East before settling in Mississippi and developing a new variety of cotton. Haller Nutt himself, who made certain improvements on Eli Whitney's cotton gin, evidently looked forward to reading his favorite Greek, Latin and Hebrew authors in the hundred-foot high rotunda of this Moorish octagonal contrived by Samuel Sloan of Philadelphia. As for Natchez itself, it was a Grecian boom town once the Natchez trace to Nashville became well-traveled. Of all the Grecian villas, the best may be Melrose, built by Judge Edward B. Turner, who must have been well informed on the subject of the murder in 1849 of the canny Free Negro barber William Johnson, whose diary tells so much of the progress of the Natchez Free Negro colony. The murderer appears to have been another Free Negro, but the state could not prove this, and such was justice in Mississippi, he was set free. This was almost as sensational a case as the killing in Ripley, not too many miles away, of Colonel William C. Falkner on November 5, 1889. Forty years before this, Falkner was acquitted of stabbing and killing a certain Robert Hindman, who had accused him of being a liar. But Falkner was not merely an expert with the knife. He was also a railroad builder and a novelist, and the preposterous plot of his *White Rose of Memphis* may have enchanted his great-grandson William Faulkner.

Louisiana has many more architectural treasures than Mississippi, although Mark Twain lost his sense of humor on contemplating the Gothic capitol, at Baton Rouge by James Harrison Dakin. "Sir Walter Scott is probably responsible," Twain claimed in *Life on the Mississippi*, "for it is not conceivable that this little sham castle would ever have been built, if he had not run the people mad, a couple of generations ago, with his mediaeval romances. The South has not yet recovered from the debilitating influences of his books. . . . By itself," he added, "the imitation castle is doubtless harmless, and well enough; but as a symbol and breeder and sustainer of maudlin Middle-Age romanticism here in the midst of the plainest and sturdiest and infinitely greatest and worthiest of all centuries the world has seen, it is necessarily a hurtful thing and a mistake."

Whether Mark Twain would have approved of the other monuments of Louisiana about to be singled out is a question. He might have been indignant at the sight of Afton Villa at Saint Francisville, remodeled in 1849, possibly by Dakin, into a subtle Gothic residence for the planter David Barrow. Would Mark Twain have excused Greenwood in Saint Francisville, the plantation house of David's cousin William Ruffin Barrow? The Doric columns of Greenwood, reflected in a stagnant pool, were an unforgettable sight until they went up in flames a few years ago. Fire has also destroyed Afton Villa.

David and William Ruffin Barrow need not be confused with their cousin and neighbor Bennet H. Barrow, who died in 1846 worth $150,000. This Barrow was an all but illiterate figure, who did know a thing or two about borrowing from banks to finance cotton and sugar crops, but whose only pastime, apart from the Saint Francisville race track, was foxhunting. He refused to believe that Negroes were qualified for Christianity. "Went to the Miss Smiths," he noted in his diary for October 11, 1844. "Nearly all their hands have run off, from pure impudence founded in their Negroes' religion." There is a long list of Negroes that Bennet H. Barrow whipped.

Here is the model, if you need one, for Tom Gordon, the unappetizing Southern white of Mrs. Stowe's *Dred*, a novel set in the North Carolina which once was the Barrows' home. Tom Gordon will always have his place in American literature. His vicious behavior provides the perfect foil for Dred himself, the son of Denmark Vesey, leader of the South Carolina black insurrection of 1822. "The burden of the beasts of the South!" cries Dred from the depths of the Great Dismal Swamp. "The land of trouble and anguish, from whence cometh the young and the old lion, the viper and the fiery, flying serpent! Go write it upon a table, and note it in a book. . . . Behold our daughters sold to be harlots!"

There is no Bennet H. Barrow to haunt Shadows on the Tèche, the plantation house at Iberia of David Weeks, whose bricks were fired by slave labor and whose Doric colonnade proves the dignity of the original owner. A more majestic Doric creation is Chrétien Point near Opelousas, built by Hyppolite Chrétien in 1831. Far more splendid is Madewood, the Corinthian seat at Napoleonville of Colonel Thomas Pugh. Pugh's architect was Henry Howard, whose great achievement was Belle Grove at White Castle. This, the most magnificent mansion in the entire South on the eve of the war, was built in 1857 for a certain John Andrews, Jr. from Virginia, about whom history is silent. Until a few years ago Belle Grove, with its Corinthian capitals and strawberry-stucco façade was the most provocative ruin in the United States. Unhappily, it was set on fire by tramps or hoodlums.

Now that Afton Villa, Greenwood and Belle Grove have vanished, there is no doubt that the only great plantation house in the vicinity of New Orleans is Oak Alley at Vacherie, whose twenty-eight

Doric columns testify to the prosperity of the planter J. T. Roman, who settled in this grove of live oaks in 1836. The owner was the brother of the distinguished Whig governor André Roman, but the name of the architect has not come down to us.

Beautiful glooms, soft dusks in the noon-day fire,
Wildwood privacies, closets of lone desire . . .

ran the hymn of Sidney Lanier to a similar grove of live oaks in Georgia.

This may be the moment to mention Parlange Plantation at New Roads, an eloquent answer to the needs of the climate that dates from 1750 when the Marquise de Ternant (whose second husband was the French naval officer Charles Parlange) moved into this one-and-one-half story cottage of cypress and mud and moss construction set above a brick basement. Its airy gallery may possibly have inspired the architect of Oak Alley eighty-six years later.

Wade Hampton III, the son of Wade of Millwood, was aware of all the architecture that we have been describing, for he made many trips into the Deep South to watch over the family properties and even made his home for a time in Linden, Mississippi. A prudent investor, he came to wonder whether slavery was economic, and was not the man to rejoice when secession came. Secession could be justified, he felt, but was it opportune?

Yet once secession was inevitable, he rallied with what looked like romantic fervor to the Lost Cause, raising mostly at his own expense a legion composed of cavalry, infantry and artillery. Wounded at First Manassas, he was appointed a Brigadier General in 1862. Later, after J. E. B. Stuart's death at Yellow Tavern, he was made commander of Lee's cavalry. So it was natural for Hampton to think of fighting on after Lee's surrender. He even dreamed of a last stand in Texas at the side of Jefferson Davis.

This heroic attitude did him no harm in South Carolina, where no one could believe Sherman's charge that he was responsible for the burning of Columbia. In 1865 he came close to being elected Governor. His chance came in 1877 when he succeeded in ousting Daniel H. Chamberlain, the last representative of reconstruction. There is no doubt that Hampton stood for White Supremacy, but he was no common bully. "We intend to try to elevate them, educate them, and show them the responsibilities as well as the blessings of liberty," he said of the Negroes. Re-elected Governor, he eventually served in the United States Senate. Yet he knew that the supremacy of the Hamptons had come to an end. In 1868 he went into bankruptcy confessing debts of $1,041,991.

"I have claimed nothing from South Carolina but a grave in yonder churchyard," he remarked shortly before his death in 1902. He was pointing to the graveyard of Trinity Church, Columbia.

Roman Catholic Cathedral, New Orleans, Louisiana, 1794 (Architect unknown).

Presbytère, New Orleans, Louisiana, 1795–1813 (architect unknown).

Cabildo, New Orleans, Louisiana, 1795 (architect unknown).

Blanc house, Bayou Saint John, New Orleans, Louisiana, 1780–1810 (architect unknown).

Cast-iron balconies on Royal Street, New Orleans, Louisiana, c. 1837 (architect unknown).

City Hall, New Orleans, Louisiana, 1857 (James Gallier, Sr.).

Residence of R. G. Robinson, New Orleans, Louisiana, 1864 (James Gallier, Jr.).

Houmas Plantation, Residence of John S. Preston, Burnside, Louisiana, 1840 (architect unknown), House and Garçonnière.

Ruins of Millwood Plantation, Residence of Wade Hampton II, Columbia, South Carolina, c. 1830 (architect unknown).

Milford, Residence of John Laurence Manning, Pinewood, South Carolina,
c. 1839 (Nathaniel F. Potter). Private.

Ingelside, Residence of Henry Boone Ingels, Lexington, Kentucky, 1852 (John McMurtry). Destroyed.

Capitol, Frankfort, Kentucky, 1827–30 (Gideon Shryock.)

*Bank of Louisville, Louisville, Kentucky, 1838 (James Harrison Dakin).
Serving in 1979 as the foyer for a local theater group.*

Loudoun, Lexington, Kentucky, 1850 (Alexander Jackson Davis and John McMurtry). Disfigured by additions not showing in this picture, the house serves today as a community center.

White Hall, Residence of Cassius Marcellus Clay, Richmond, Kentucky, c. 1865 (Thomas Lewinski). Now a state shrine.

Capitol, Nashville, Tennessee, 1854 (William Strickland).

Belmont, Residence of Joseph Acklen, Nashville, Tennessee, 1850 (William Strickland?). Serving in 1978 as the headquarters of Ward-Belmont College.

Belle Meade, Residence of William Giles Harding, Nashville, Tennessee, 1853, (William Strickland?). Open, Association for the Preservation of Tennessee Antiquities.

Rattle & Snap, Residence of George Polk, Columbia, Tennessee, 1845, (architect unknown).

Residence of Gideon Pillow, Columbia Tennessee, c. 1840 (architect unknown).

Offices of Gideon Pillow, Columbia, Tennessee, c. 1840 (architect unknown).

Barton Academy, Mobile, Alabama, 1835–36 (J. H. & C. B. Dakin).

Government Street Presbyterian Church, Mobile, Alabama, 1837, (J. H. & C. B. Dakin).

*Forks of Cypress, Residence of James Jackson, Florence, Alabama, 1820?,
(architect unknown). Destroyed.*

Gaineswood, Residence of Nathan Bryan Whitfield Demopolis, Alabama, 1842 (architect unknown). Open, Alabama Department of Conservation.

Residence of John Calhoun Edwards, Opelika, Alabama, c. 1865 (architect unknown).

Ruins of Windsor, Residence of Smith C. Daniel, Port Gibson, Mississippi, 1861 (architect unknown).

Residence of Dr. Charles Bonner, Holly Springs, Mississippi, 1858 (architect unknown).

Longwood, Residence of Haller Nutt, Natchez, Mississippi, 1860 (Samuel Sloan). Private but open.

Melrose, Residence of Edward C. Turner, Natchez, Mississippi, c. 1840 (architect unknown). Open by appointment.

Capitol, Baton Rouge, Louisiana, 1847–50 (James Harrison Dakin).

Afton Villa, Residence of David Barrow, Saint Francisville, Louisiana, 1849 (James Harrison Dakin?). Destroyed.

Greenwood, Residence of William Ruffin Barrow, Saint Francisville, Louisiana, 1830 (architect unknown). Destroyed.

*Shadows on the Tèche, Residence of David Weeks, New Iberia, Louisiana,
1830 (architect unknown). Open, National Trust.*

Chrétien Point, Residence of Hyppolite Chrétien, Opelousas, Louisiana, c. 1831 (architect unknown).

Madewood, Residence of Thomas Pugh, Napoleonville, Louisiana, 1848 (Henry Howard). Open.

Ruins of Belle Grove, Residence of John Andrews, White Castle, Louisiana,
1857 (Henry Howard). Destroyed.

Oak Alley, Residence of J. T. Roman, Vacherie, Louisiana, 1830 (architect unknown). Open.

Parlange, Residence of the Marquise de Ternant, New Roads, Louisiana, c. 1750 (architect unknown). Open.

Trinity Church Cathedral, Columbia, South Carolina, 1840 (E. B. White).

THE NEW SOUTH

"When I found myself on my feet," Henry Woodfin Grady recalled, "every nerve in my body was strung as tight as a fiddle-string, and all tingling. I knew then that I had a message for that assemblage, and as soon as I opened my mouth, it came rushing out."

The time was December 21, 1886, the occasion the annual meeting of the New England Club of New York, and young Grady of the *Atlanta Constitution* had been asked to talk on the New South. In the audience sat William Tecumseh Sherman.

"I want to say to General Sherman," Grady began, "who is considered an able man in our parts, though some people think he is a kind of careless man about fire, that from the ashes he left us in 1864 we have raised a brave and beautiful city.

"What is the sum of our work?" he asked. "We have found out that in the summing up the Free Negro counts more than he did as a slave. We have planted the schoolhouse on the hilltop and made it free to white and black. . . .

"The New South," he went on, "is enamored of her new work. Her soul is stirred with the breath of a new life. . . . We have learned that one Northern immigrant is worth fifty foreigners, and have smoothed the path to southward, wiped out the place where Mason and Dixon's Line used to be, and hung out the latchstring to you and yours."

Northern capital was more than welcome. "We shall," he explained to a crowd at Augusta, Georgia in 1887, "secure from the North more friendliness and sympathy, more champions and friends, through the influence of our industrial growth, than through political aspiration or achievement."

This was Grady's modern message. He was not always so modern. He believed in "the clear and unmistakable domination of the white race in the South," as he made plain to George Washington Cable, the author of *The Grandissimes*. "Each race obeys its instinct and congregates about its own centers. At the theater they sit in opposite sections of the same gallery. Each worships in his own church, and educates his children in his own schools."

Grady's prayer for prosperity was answered in Atlanta, ultimately of course in Houston and Dallas. In Atlanta he was one of the allies of the brothers John

Hamilton and Samuel Martin Inman of Tennessee, formidable cotton brokers who invested not only in Tennessee Coal & Iron and the Louisville and Nashville Railroad, but also in the *Atlanta Constitution*. In Atlanta the ultimate contribution of the Inmans to architecture could be measured by the Renaissance mansion of Edward Hamilton Inman, nephew of the Inmans just mentioned, built in 1928. This was the work of Philip Trammel Schutze, who did not need to be reminded of the accomplishments of Stanford White and Charles Adams Platt twenty-five years before this in the North.*

Texas, however, may tell us more than Georgia about the outward and visible signs of the prosperity that Grady longed for. In Austin the railroad financier Colonel Edward Mandell House, later the master mind of the Wilson Administration, called on Frank Freeman of Brooklyn to design him in 1891 a mansion in the so-called Shingle Style that Richardson and McKim, Mead & White had made so popular. This has been destroyed to make way for a parking lot, but it once testified that Texans had taste.

The port of Galveston, before the hurricane of 1900 and the building of the ship canal to Houston cancelled its strategic importance, may not be neglected. It was an ambitious town as early as 1838 when its founder the fur trader of French descent Michael Menard built himself a handsome Greek Revival house that is still standing. In the Grady era the vigorous Nicholas J. Clayton, who may have admired the work of the Southerner Richardson in New England, planned a castle for Congressman Walter Gresham in 1888 that came close to proclaiming that Galveston would one day have its own steamship line to Barcelona. Possibly, quite possibly, Clayton was responsible for the fanciful frame house in 1887 of the

* Quite as conservative as the Inman mansion was the campus of Duke University at Durham, North Carolina, financed by the tobacco millionaire James B. Duke, who selected the widow of an Atlanta Inman as his second wife. This half-Tudor Gothic, half-Georgian commission was the work c 1925–1927 of the office of Horace Trumbauer of Philadelphia. Trumbauer stayed far away from the drafting board. To what employee he surrendered this commission is not known, but the most distinguished designer on his staff was the Black Julien Abele, who may have planned Duke's glorious evocation of eighteenth-century Bordeaux at Fifth Avenue and Seventy-eighth Street, New York City.

wholesale dry goods merchant Jacob Sonnentheil. For Sonnentheil was a partner in Greenleve, Block & Company, who chose Clayton for the architect of their business building.

The time may now have come to consider the list of Northern millionaires who answered, each in his own way, Grady's appeal for Northern capital in the South. That the climate was congenial was understood by George Washington Vanderbilt, the grandson of the Commodore, whose gigantic Biltmore, landscaped by Frederick Law Olmsted, was completed in 1895 by Richard Morris Hunt. The foundations of this château at Asheville, North Carolina, vaster than certain of the models from the Loire Valley, covered five acres, and Henry James, so often critical of the monuments of our millionaires, was forced to admit that here was "a thing of the high Rothschild manner." Incidentally, it was a thing that worried other members of the Vanderbilt family. George, who inherited only $10,000,000 from his father, was so fond of this project that he went into his capital to complete it. This was rash, thought George's brother-in-law Hamilton McKown Twombly.

But no Northerner responded to Grady with more loyalty than John D. Rockefeller's partner Henry M. Flagler, who sold one block after another of Standard Oil to make of Florida, which had been a wilderness, a paradise for vacationers. True, there were Northerners who sought out Saint Augustine in winter before Flagler worked his will. One of these was teen-age Julia Newberry, the daughter of the Astors' advance agent in Chicago, who was not too impressed by the Longworths of Cincinnati in 1870, and pronounced the town "a queer place, and its charm lies in being queer."

Another Northerner in Saint Augustine was the novelist Constance Fenimore Woolson. Henry James noted the "high appreciation of orange gardens and white beaches, pine barrens, and rivers smothered in jungles" in her *East Angels,* an idyll of pre-Flagler Florida, but failed to respond to her passionate friendship. On January 24, 1894 Miss Woolson fell to her death from a window in Venice.

"Saint Augustine in the winter is full of grandees, you know," she wrote on one of her happy days to the Southern poet Paul Hamilton Hayne. "By grandees I mean scions of those old New York City families who come from the Dutch times and have *Van* in their names somewhere; people who have been

rich for generations and absolutely know nothing of their own country outside of the *City* although very familiar of course with Europe. Several of these gentlemen I know quite well. This is what one said: *Dickens? Yes—I know; some people like his works, but I do not: they are very low. I never care to read about the lower classes. . . .* These are the people who make it a point to travel with *portable baths* always, in charge of their valets. They have only two adjectives, *nice* and *beastly*—I am always getting into quarrels with them. And yet they have spoiled me for any other kind of society, almost—they are so (to use their own word) *nice,* in a great many ways after all . . .

"I must hurry down among the grandees and hear some good music again," she continued. "I shall come fresh from the desert into the ring again, and hear that *flounces are worn very flat now,* and that *Miss Rhineland is not engaged after all* and that *Mrs. Van-Something is as silly as ever with her five poodle dogs.* Won't it be refreshing? And then when the wind blows, they will say *it is a nasty day.* And they will all take immensely long walks English fashion, and growl because they cannot have their beef rare. And really, Mr. Hayne, what *is* the reason we can never have our beef rare down here?"

Such was the genteel world that Flagler destroyed. The son of a Presbyterian minister from Hammondsport, New York, he had known what it was to be poor. Yet he was just the man to understand that Northern vacationers must have their beef rare. He had drawn almost all of Rockefeller's contracts.

"If it weren't for Florida," he once complained, "I'd be a rich man today." He was so impressed by his first visit to Saint Augustine in 1883 that he began building the Ponce de León Hotel there in 1885. When it opened in 1888, it was the most exuberant hotel in the United States. No better advertisement could be imagined for the architects John Merven Carrère and Thomas Hastings. Hastings' father had been the pastor of the West Presbyterian Church in New York, where Flagler was a faithful parishioner, but there was nothing Presbyterian about the Ponce de León, whose irresistible Spanish atmosphere owed much to the playful imagination of Carrère & Hastings's assistant Bernard R. Maybeck. When it was rumored that a good chef might be dismissed from the Ponce, Flagler proved that he could live up to his architects' standards. "Hire another cook and two more orchestras," came the word from on high.

In the meantime he asked Carrère & Hastings to design the Flagler Memorial Church with its manse and Grace Church for Methodist visitors to the resort.

"I believe," Flagler used to say, "this state is the easiest place for many men to gain a living. I do not believe anyone else will develop it if I do not. I believe," he reminded his pastor, "it's a thousand times better than your colleges and universities, but I do hope to live long enough to prove I am a good businessman by getting a dividend on my investment."

This he did. Before his death in 1913 he succeeded in running the Florida East Coast Railway all the way to Key West, besides building other hotels in Miami and Palm Beach. He made his home in Palm Beach, where Carrère & Hastings built him a palace that was no more inviting than a coffin. At least there was no hint of the talent they displayed in the Jefferson Hotel in Richmond or in the New York Public Library.

"Ninety-five per cent of them love money, not me," Flagler remarked of those who idolized him at the end of his career. "He craved companionship," said his pastor at the memorial service, "yet always claimed he could not win it. Badly as he wanted to, he could not let himself go. In his later life you frequently saw him with the little white dog that rode with him in his chair. I have seen him for moments at a time with his face buried in little Bobby's fur talking to him like a father to his child."

Flagler's only rival in exploiting Florida was Henry Bradley Plant, the master of the Atlantic Coast Line, who startled Tampa in 1891 by opening the Tampa Bay Hotel, a marvelous Moorish fantasy by J. A. Wood. In 1979 this serves as the University of Tampa. And the Ponce de León has been converted into Flagler College.

James Deering of International Harvester had no idea of improving the Southern economy in the manner of Flagler and Plant. Like George Vanderbilt, he was searching for a playground. A fastidious bachelor suffering all his life from pernicious anaemia, he played next to no role in the farm machinery business, devoting himself instead to the art objects he religiously collected in Europe. Villa Vizcaya, his palace on Biscayne Bay, Miami, may be said to have begun the day the decorator Elsie de Wolfe introduced him to the art critic Paul Chalfin. Chalfin was to be his guide on his trips to Europe, but the palace itself, vaguely recalling Baldassare Longhena's Villa Rezzonico on the Brenta, was the work of F. Burrall

Hoffman, aided by the landscape architect Diego Suarez. The great care that Hoffman took in 1914 in creating the perfect setting for Deering's acquisitions has only been really appreciated since 1952, when Villa Vizcaya, like Biltmore, was turned into a museum.

As for John D. Rockefeller, Jr., he was as serious as Flagler in his designs upon the South. Educated by William A. R. Goodwin, the rector of Bruton Parish Church at Williamsburg, in the importance of restoring the colonial capital of Virginia, he kept his plans a secret until June 12, 1928, when the Williamsburg Holding Company appointed the firm of Perry, Shaw & Hepburn to superintend the project. Williamsburg may be criticized by certain visitors who miss the *golden stain of time*—opinions will always differ as to the value of any restoration, no matter how competent—but Colonial Williamsburg is not merely a re-invention of a vanished past. It is also a center for studies on the colonial period. Moreover, travelers may also see the real thing touched by time, the Rockefellers having recently opened nearby Carter's Grove to the public. One concession to the twentieth century has been made: the industrial designer George Nelson planned the Information Center.

Whether Grady would have been pleased by the prowess of Addison Mizner, who turned up in Palm Beach in 1918 on a stretcher, aged forty-five, is questionable. But Mizner, in spite of the fact that the doctors had given him up before he caught his first sight of what would become Worth Avenue, had just what it took to invent the setting that was so appealing in later days to the Duke and Duchess of Windsor. "He is always cheerful and hearty," said his good friend Paris Singer of the sewing machine family, "and his mastery of tavern English is a joy to everybody within hearing." He stretched at his prime six feet two and weighed two hundred fifty pounds. This made him an impressive figure in the eyes of Mrs. Hugh Dillman, the former Mrs. Horace Dodge of Grosse Pointe, and many other Northerners who set the fashion during the Florida land boom of the 1920s. Or did Mizner set *their* fashion? "What I really did was to turn the Spanish inside out like a glove, making all the openings face a patio or a courtyard" he claimed, adding that "most modern architects have spent their lives carrying out a period to the last letter and producing a characteristic copybook effect."

He could be bland, as in the Alhambra-like court-yard he contrived in 1919 for Paris Singer's Ever-glades Club. He could also be vainglorious, as in the Palm Beach houses of Mrs. Dillman and Mrs. Stotes-bury, both of which have been pulled down. "Pop," he bragged one day to his painting contractor, "I want this to look a thousand years old," and filled a bucket with burning tar paper to smoke up the ceiling of the first house he built for himself. Woodwork had to be aged, and as quickly as possible, so wormholes were often jabbed in with icepicks.

His was an ephemeral world and he knew it, cashing in on his commissions with the joy of a playwright the morning after a hit. He and his brother are supposed to have sold $11,000,000 in lots the day they launched their Boca Raton development. This was to collapse at the end of the land boom, although the Cloister, his club at Boca, survives today as part of the immense Boca Raton Hotel. He could never be serene, like his rival from Switzerland Maurice Fatio, whose own house on Highway A1.A and that of the banker Mortimer L. Schiff of Kuhn, Loeb remain palaces as confident as almost any masterpiece by Charles Platt. Mizner was to die insolvent in 1933, but left us Worth Avenue and the Clubhouse of the apparently substantial Gulf Stream Club. Here his inspiration was obvious: the horseshoe staircase of the château of Fontainebleau.

He could never be threatening like Maurice Lapidus, the inventor of the Americana, Eden Roc and Fontainebleau hotels at Miami Beach. The most famous of these was the latter, completed in 1954 and destined for bankruptcy in 1977. "When Hollywood wanted to make the ultimate romantic movie about Miami Beach, *Goldfinger*, the James Bond movie, the ultimate escapist picture, they needed a gorgeous setting for spies and girls," said Lapidus's son. "They had the set already made for them, the Fontaine-bleau."

Lapidus, a Russian-born graduate of the Columbia University School of Architecture, got his start drawing acanthus leaves for Warren & Wetmore's New York Central Building on Park Avenue. From this he moved on to designing shops like the Parisian Bootery in New York. But hotels were to be his specialty, and he knew how to get on with hotel promoters. "When I started the Fontainebleau, it was going to be contemporary," he has told us. "Once and for all I was going to design a beautiful contemporary interior. I drew the first sketches and

the owner said, *You must be crazy. I don't want this. I want French Provincial.* When I heard this, I felt sick. So I took out some pictures of French Provincial, and I said, *Is this what you want?* He said, *Oh, my God, not that old-fashioned French Provincial. I want that nice modern French Provincial.* Now, try and solve that. . . . My client was just as illiterate and uncultured as many of his guests. I was faced with a problem." The problem did not embarrass him. "You do not object to kitsch?" Lapidus was asked. "Kitsch is the word," came the answer. "I never felt that I was a status architect. I resolved early in my career that, since I probably would not leave my mark, I might as well enjoy what I'm doing."

One of the gimmicks of the Fontainebleau was its "Getting-To-Know-You Room," where boys and girls of all ages could learn to make friends. To design a hotel in 1979 without any such come-ons is apparently an invitation to failure. One expert at come-ons is John Calvin Portman, Jr., a native of Walhalla, South Carolina. Named Outstanding Young Man of the Year by the Georgia Chamber of Commerce in 1959, and Salesman of the Year by the Sales and Marketing Executives of Atlanta in 1968, he came to the notice of the Pritzker family of Chicago, backers of the ever-expanding chain of Hyatt hotels, not long after his graduation from the Georgia Institute of Technology.

"It's hard to sell just a pillow," admitted Hugo M. Friend, Jr., the president of the Hyatt Corporation. "You have to sell some sizzle, too." This was a message that Portman understood. He could not object when Friend made plain that "hotels are too expensive for mere mortals to build." Friend was talking in terms of rooms running from $50,000 to $70,000 each in construction costs, a challenge that Portman met in 1967 when he completed the Hyatt Regency in Atlanta, whose glass-cage elevators spinning up to horrendous heights in an atrium that denied such a thing as human scale made an immediate impact on the tourist trade. Who knows, Portman may have found his inspiration in the dramatic sketches for buildings never built by the Italian Futurist Antonio Sant'Elia fifty years before.

Henry Grady would have been bound to approve of Chicago capital in downtown Atlanta, and would have relished Portman's success in the North. San Francisco has surrendered to Portman, and so has Detroit, where Henry Ford II encouraged the erection of the tremendous lobby and neighboring towers of the Detroit Plaza Hotel in the Renaissance Center. Whether Portman will be honored in the future is an unanswered question. He may not be half so shrewed in solving the practical problems of his profession as the late Benjamin Marshall, whose Drake Hotel in Chicago has already celebrated fifty-eight years of prosperity.

The prosperous South that Grady prayed for has given us, however, more than Portman. Modern architecture with a capital M may be seen in the South of today. In 1926 the laundry operator G. B. Cooley of Monroe, Louisiana built a remarkable house by Frank Lloyd Wright's associate Walter Burley Griffin, complete with the subtle cove lighting that was one of Griffin's trade marks. The plans had been drawn back in 1912, before Griffin won the competition for the plan of Canberra, Australia, which led to his practicing in Australia and India the rest of his life.

Wright himself has not been neglected. In 1940 he got the chance to design Auldbrass, a frame house on the edge of a cypress swamp in Yemassee, South Carolina for the engineer Leigh Stevens. This was one of the unusual Wright houses of that decade, its ornament an echo of what the most ingenious carpenters accomplished in the heyday of the Gothic Revival a century before.

Grady would certainly have applauded the determination of Ludd Myrl Spivey, the Methodist minister from Eclectic, Alabama, who rescued Florida Southern College at Lakeland from insignificance by calling on Wright to plan its campus. In the end other architects were to make their appearance, but by 1940 Wright's Pfeiffer Chapel was completed, by 1942 his Roux Library and by 1948 his Administration Building. These were fantasies as congenial to the Florida climate as the Ponce de León Hotel. Finally Wright was to deal as only he could with architecture as sculpture in the Kalita Humphreys Theater of 1960 in Dallas, named for a local actress. Nearby is his vast and vastly successful mansion for the geologist John A. Gillin.

Among the other modern buildings are Eero Saarinen's magnificent John Foster Dulles Airport at Chantilly, Virginia; Ludwig Miës van der Rohe's Cullinan Hall for the Houston Museum; and the recent Pennzoil Place in Houston for the Pennzoil Company. The ominous glass towers of this skyscraper by Philip Johnson and John Burgee are a welcome variation from the omnipresent curtain walls that have become the curse of our cities in 1978. Perhaps Grady was mistaken when he claimed in 1887 that "the last hope of the old-fashioned on this continent will be lodged in the South."

But must there be no difference between architecture North and South? One problem that remains to be solved is that of a modern *regional* architecture. The use of steel and concrete might be discouraged by any architect who hopes to invent something particularly adapted to the climate, and glass, this goes without saying, should really not dominate a Southern façade. There are times when a backward glance may enrich the future. Verandas and high ceilings may do more for comfort than the most efficient air conditioning. Possibly, quite possibly, frame structures may be built as practical as the Hext house in Beaufort, Oak Alley or Parlange.

We may learn from the past without being so silly as to reproduce it.

Swan House, Residence of E. H. Inman, Atlanta, Georgia, 1928 (Philip T. Schutze.) Open, Atlanta Historical Society.

*Residence of Colonel E. M. House, Austin Texas, c. 1891 (Frank Freeman)
Destroyed.*

Residence of Michael B. Menard, Galveston, Texas, 1838 (architect unknown).

Residence of Walter Gresham, Galveston, Texas, 1888 (Nicholas J. Clayton). Open. Newman Center, University of Texas.

Residence of Jacob Sonnentheil, Galveston, Texas, 1887 (Nicholas J. Clayton?).

Biltmore, Residence of George Washington Vanderbilt II, Asheville, North Carolina, 1895 (Richard Morris Hunt). Open, Mr. William A. V. Cecil.

Grace Methodist Church, Saint Augustine, Florida, 1887 (Carrère & Hastings).

Two views of Hotel Ponce de León, Saint Augustine, Florida, 1885–88, (Carrère & Hastings) In 1979 maintained by Flagler College.

Residence of Henry Morrison Flagler, Palm Beach, Florida, 1901 (Carrère & Hastings).

Tampa Bay Hotel, Tampa, Florida, 1891 (J. A. Wood). In 1979 Tampa College.

Exterior and stone barge, Villa Vizcaya, Residence of James Deering, Miami, Florida, 1914–17 (F. Burrall Hoffman and Diego Suarez). Open, Metropolitan Dade County Park and Recreation Department.

Governor's Palace, Williamsburg, Virginia, 1706–20 (architect unknown).
Open, Colonial Williamsburg.

Bruton Parish Church, Williamsburg, Virginia, 1710–15 (architect unknown). Open, Colonial Williamsburg.

Capitol, Williamsburg, Virginia, 1705 (architect unknown). Open, Colonial Williamsburg.

Courtyard, Everglades Club, Palm Beach, Florida, 1919 (Addison Mizner).

Residence of Maurice Fatio, Palm Beach, Florida, c. 1924 (Maurice Fatio).

Residence of Mortimer Schiff, Palm Beach, Florida, c. 1924 (Maurice Fatio).

Hotel Fontainebleau, Miami Beach, Florida, 1954 (Morris Lapidus).

Lobby, Hyatt Regency Hotel, Atlanta, Georgia, 1967 (John Calvin Portman, Jr. (The sculptural screen is by Richard Lippold).

Residence of G. B. Cooley, Monroe, Louisiana, 1912–26 (Walter Burley Griffin).

Auldbrass, Residence of Leigh Stevens, Yemassee, South Carolina, 1940 (Frank Lloyd Wright).

Administration Building, Florida Southern College, Lakeland, Florida, 1948
(Frank Lloyd Wright).

Exterior and Interior, Kalita Humphreys Theater, Dallas, Texas, 1960,
(Frank Lloyd Wright).

Cullinan Hall, Houston Museum, Houston, Texas, 1958 (Ludwig Miës van der Rohe).

John Foster Dulles Airport, Chantilly, Virginia, 1963 (Eero Saarinen Associates).

Pennzoil Place, Houston, Texas, 1975 (Philip Johnson and John Burgee).

BIBLIOGRAPHY

Abernethy, Thomas P., *Three Virginia Frontiers*, Baton Rouge, 1940

Adams, William D., ed., et al., *The Eye of Jefferson*, Washington, 1976

Alexander, Drury B., *Texas Homes of the Nineteenth Century*, Austin, 1968

Armes, Ethel M., *Stratford Hall*, Richmond, 1936

Arthur, Stanley C., et al., *Old Families of Louisiana*, New Orleans, 1931

Barnstone, Howard, *The Galveston That Was*, New York, 1966

Bassett, John S., ed., *The Writings of Colonel William Byrd*, New York, 1901

Beirne, Rosamund R., et al., *William Buckland*, Baltimore, 1958

Bowes, Frederick P., *The Culture of Early Charleston*, Chapel Hill, 1942

Bridenbaugh, Carl, *Myths and Realities*, Baton Rouge, 1951

———, *Seat of Empire*, Williamsburg, 1950.

Brock, Henry I., *Colonial Churches in Virginia*, Richmond, 1930

Bruce, Philip A., *History of the University of Virginia*, 5 v., Charlottesville, 1920

Bruce, William C., *Recollections*, Baltimore, 1936

Cauthen, Charles W., ed., *Family Letters of the Three Wade Hamptons*, Columbia, 1953

Chastellux, Marquis de, *Voyages dans l'Amérique Septentrionale*, 2 v., Paris, 1786

Chopin, Kate, *The Awakening*, New York, 1972 (several modern editions)

Cochran, Gifford A., *Grandeur in Tennessee*, New York, 1946

Cook, John W., et al., *Conversations with Architects*, New York, 1973

Couper, William, *One Hundred Years at VMI*, 4 v., Richmond, 1939

Craven, Avery, *Edmund Ruffin, Southerner*, New York, 1932

Curtis, Nathaniel C., *New Orleans*, Philadelphia, 1933

Da Costa, Beverley, ed., *Historic Houses of America Open to the Public*, New York, 1971

Davis, Alexander J., Correspondence, Print Room, Metropolitan Museum, New York

Davis, Edwin A., ed., *Plantation Life in the Florida Parishes of Louisiana*, New York, 1943

——— and Horgan, William R., *The Barber of Natchez*, Baton Rouge, 1954

Deas, Anne I., ed., *Correspondence of Mr. Ralph Izard*, Vol. 1, New York, 1844

DeForest, John W., *Miss Ravenel's Conversion from Secession to Loyalty*, New York, 1867 (also several modern editions)

Drayton, John, *A View of South Carolina*, Charleston, 1802

Eaton, Clement, *The Mind of the Old South*, Baton Rouge, 1967

Edel, Leon, *Henry James: The Middle Years*, New York, 1962

Falkner, William C., *The White Rose of Memphis*, New York, 1953

Farish, Hunter D., ed., *Journal and Letters of Philip Vickers Fithian*, Williamsburg, 1943

Flagler, Henry Morrison: In Memoriam, n. p., 1914

Gallagher, Helen M. P., *Robert Mills*, New York, 1935

Gallier, James, *Autobiography of James Gallier*, Paris, 1864

Gilchrist, Agnes A., *William Strickland*, Philadelphia, 1950

Glen, Thomas A., *Some Colonial Mansions*, 2 v., Philadelphia, 1898

Gray, David, *Thomas Hastings, Architect*, New York, 1933

Gray, Lewis C., *History of Agriculture in the Southern United States*, 2 v., New York, 1941

Greene, E. L., "Some Early Columbians," *The State*, July 10, 1930

Hamlin, Talbot F., *Benjamin Henry Latrobe*, New York, 1955

———, *Greek Revival Architecture in America*, New York, 1944

Hammond, Ralph C., *Ante Bellum Mansions of Alabama*, New York, 1951

Harris, Joel C., ed., *H. W. Grady: Writings and Speeches*, New York, 1890

Haskins, Charles H., "The Yazoo Land Companies," *American Historical Review*, Vol. 5, Part 2.

Hendrick, Burton J., *The Lees of Virginia*, Boston, 1935

Hill, Helen, *George Mason*, Cambridge, 1938

Hodson, Peter, "The Design and Building of Bremo," Masters Thesis in Architectural History, University of Virginia, 1967

Hooker, Richard J., ed., *The Carolina Backcountry on the Eve of the Revolution*, Chapel Hill, 1953

Hubbell, Jay R., ed., "Some New Letters of Constance Fenimore Woolson," *New England Quarterly*, December, 1941

Irving, John B., *The South Carolina Jockey Club*, Charleston, 1857

Johnston, Alva, "The Palm Beach Architect," *The New Yorker*, November 22 and 29, December 6 and 13, 1952

Kibler, Lilian A., *Benjamin F. Perry*, Durham, 1946

Kimball, Fiske, "The Building of Bremo," *Virginia Magazine of History and Biography*, January, 1949

———, *Thomas Jefferson, Architect*, Boston, 1916

———, and Caraway, Gertrude S., "Tryon's Palace," *New-York Historical Society*, *Quarterly Bulletin*, January, 1940

Kimball, Marie, *Jefferson: The Scene of Europe, 1784–1789*, New York, 1950

Konkle, Burton A., *John Motley Morehead*, Philadelphia, 1922

Lancaster, Clay, *Ante Bellum Houses of the Bluegrass*, Lexington, 1961

———, *Back Streets and Pine Trees*, Lexington, 1956

———, "Three Gothic Revival Houses of Lexington," *American Collector*, December, 1948

LaRochefoucauld-Liancourt, Duc de, *Voyage dans les Etats-Unis d'Amérique*, 8 v., Paris, 1798–99

Laughlin, Clarence J., *Ghosts Along the Mississippi*, New York, 1948

Lefèvre, Edwin, "Flagler and Florida," *Everybody's*, February, 1910

Lincoln, F. S., *Charleston: A Photographic Study*, New York, 1946

Lindsey, Robert, "Hyatt's Kingdom of Rooms," *New York Times*, August 29, 1976

Logan, Rayford W., ed., *Life and Times of Frederick Douglass*, New York, 1962

Lyon, Elizabeth A. M., *Atlanta Architecture: The Victorian Heritage*, Atlanta, 1976

Maher, James T., *The Twilight of Splendor*, Boston, 1975

Malone, Dumas, *Jefferson and the Ordeal of Liberty*, Boston, 1962

Martin, John W., *Henry M. Flagler*, New York, 1956

McCrady, Edward, *History of South Carolina under the Royal Government*, New York, 1899

McWhiney, Grady, *Southerners and Other Americans*, New York, 1973

Meade, William, *Old Churches, Ministers and Families of Virginia*, Philadelphia, 1861

Merritt, Elizabeth, *James Henry Hammond*, Baltimore, 1923

"The Milford Papers," *Newsletter, Victorian Society in America*, Winter, 1973

Morison, Hugh S., *Early American Architecture*, New York, 1952

Morton, Louis, *Robert Carter of Nomini Hall*, Williamsburg, 1941

Nevins, Allan, *John D. Rockefeller*, 2 v., New York, 1940

Newberry, Julia R., *The Diary of Julia Newberry*, New York, 1933

Newcomb, Rexford G., *Architecture in Old Kentucky*, Urbana, 1953

Nichols, Frederick, *The Architecture of Georgia*, Savannah, 1977

———, *The Early Architecture of Georgia*, Chapel Hill, 1957

Nolte, Vincent, *Fifty Years in Both Hemispheres*, London, 1854

Oliphant, Mary C. Simms, et al., eds., *The Letters of William Gilmore Simms*, 5 v., Columbia, 1952–56

Orr, Christina, *Addison Mizner*, Palm Beach, 1977

Phillips, Ulrich B., *Life and Labor in the Old South*, Boston, 1939

Quincy, Josiah, Jr., "Journal, 1773," *Proceedings, Massachusetts Historical Society*, Volume 49

Randall, Henry S., *Life of Thomas Jefferson*, 3 v., New York, 1858

Ravenel, Beatrice S. J., *Architects of Charleston*, Charleston, 1945

Ravenel, Harriott H., *Charleston: The Place and the People*, New York, 1906

———, *Eliza Pinckney*, New York, 1896

Reniers, Percival, *The Springs of Virginia*, Chapel Hill, 1941

"The Restoration of Colonial Williamsburg," *Architectural Record*, December, 1935

Russell, William H., *My Diary North and South*, Boston, 1863

Sale, Edith T., *Manors of Virginia in Colonial Times*, Philadelphia, 1909

Sawyer, Elizabeth H., et al., *The Old in New Atlanta*, Atlanta, 1975

Scarborough, William K., ed., *Diary of Edmund Ruffin*, Vol. 1, Baton Rouge, 1971

Scully, Arthur, Jr., *James Dakin, Architect*, Baton Rouge, 1973

Sitterson, J. Carlyle, *Sugar Country*, Lexington, 1953

Smith, Alice H., et al., *Dwelling Houses of Charleston*, Philadelphia, 1917

Smith, J. Frazier, *White Pillars*, New York, 1941

Smyth, G. Hutchinson, *Life of H. B. Plant*, New York, 1898

Stoney, Samuel G., *Plantations of the South Carolina Low Country*, Charleston, 1938

Stowe, Harriet Beecher, *Dred: A Tale of the Great Dismal Swamp*, 2 v., Boston, 1856

———, *Uncle Tom's Cabin*, New York, 1964 (several modern editions)

Tarbell, Ida M., *Florida Architecture of Addison Mizner*, New York, 1928

Tilghman, J. Donnell, "Wye House," *Maryland Historical Magazine*, June, 1953

Tilghman, Oswald, *History of Talbot County, Maryland*, 2 v., Baltimore, 1915

Townsend, William H., *The Lion of White Hall*, Dunwoody, 1967

Tucker, Nathaniel B., *The Partisan Leader*, Saddle River, 1968

Wall, Charles C., *Mount Vernon: An Illustrated Handbook*, Mount Vernon, 1974

Wallace, David D., *Life of Henry Laurens*, New York, 1918

———, *South Carolina: A Short History*, Chapel Hill, 1951

Waterman, Thomas T., *Domestic Colonial Architecture of Tidewater Virginia*, New York, 1932

———, *The Early Architecture of North Carolina*, Chapel Hill, 1941

Wellman, Manly W., *Giant in Gray*, New York, 1949

Wertenbaker, Thomas J., *Patrician and Plebeian in Virginia*, Charlottesville, 1910

————, *The Planters of Colonial Virginia*, Princeton, 1922

Whiffin, Marcus, *Eighteenth Century Houses of Colonial Williamsburg*, Williamsburg, 1970

————, The Public Buildings of Williamsburg, Williamsburg, 1958

White, Laura A., *Robert Barnwell Rhett*, Gloucester, 1965

Williams, Ben Ames, ed., Mary B. Chesnut: *Diary from Dixie*, Boston, 1961

Wilson, Samuel, Jr., et al., *New Orleans Architecture*, 5 v., Gretna, 1971–77

Wilstach, Paul, *Mount Vernon*, New York, 1916

Woodfin, Maude H., ed., *Another Secret Diary of William Byrd of Westover*, Richmond, 1942

Woodward, C. Vann, *Origins of the New South*, Baton Rouge, 1951

————, *Tom Watson: Agrarian Rebel*, New York, 1938

Woolson, Constance Fenimore, *East Angels*, New York, 1886

Wright, Louis B., *The First Gentlemen of Virginia*, San Marino, 1940

————, ed., *The Letters of Robert Carter, 1720–27*, San Marino, 1940

INDEX (ARCHITECTS IN ITALICS)

WAYNE ANDREWS

Wayne Andrews was born in Kenilworth, Illinois, in 1913. He has been Archives of American Art Professor at Wayne State University since 1964. A graduate of Harvard, he earned his doctorate under Allan Nevins at Columbia. He was formerly Curator of Manuscripts at the New-York Historical Society and an editor at Charles Scribner's Sons; he was chosen Phi Beta Kappa Visiting Lecturer in 1975-6. He is the author of many books, including four companion volumes to the present one: *Architecture in America, Architecture in Chicago and Mid-America, Architecture in New York* and *Architecture in New England; American Gothic* is an examination of the Gothic Revival in modern architecture; other books in American history include *The Vanderbilt Legend* and *Battle for Chicago;* he has also written *Germaine*, a biography of Madame de Staël, and a study of German literature and history, *Siegfried's Curse: The German Journey from Nietzsche to Hesse*. Mr. Andrews has contributed to such publications as *The Architectural Review, Town and Country, Harper's Bazaar* and *The New York Times*.